ONE- AND TWO-STEP PROBLEMS

GLOBE FEARON EDUCATIONAL PUBLISHER
A Division of Simon & Schuster
Upper Saddle River, New Jersey

Executive Editor: Barbara Levadi
Editors: Bernice Golden, Lynn Kloss, Robert McIlwaine, Kirsten Richert
Production Manager: Penny Gibson
Production Editor: Walt Niedner
Interior Design: The Wheetley Company
Electronic Page Production: Curriculum Concepts
Cover Design: Pat Smythe

Printed in the United States of America 2 3 4 5 6 7 8 9 10 99 98

ISBN 0-8359-1539-5

GLOBE FEARON EDUCATIONAL PUBLISHER
A Division of Simon & Schuster
Upper Saddle River, New Jersey

CONTENTS

TO THE STUDENT

Access to Math is a series of 15 books designed to help you learn new skills and practice these skills in mathematics. You'll learn the steps necessary to solve a range of mathematical problems.

LESSONS HAVE THE FOLLOWING FEATURES:

❖ Lessons are easy to use. Many begin with a sample problem from a real-life experience. After the sample problem is introduced, you are taught step-by-step how to find the answer. Examples show you how to use your skills.

❖ The *Guided Practice* section demonstrates how to solve a problem similar to the sample problem. Answers are given in the first part of the problem to help you find the final answer.

❖ The *Exercises* section gives you the opportunity to practice the skill presented in the lesson.

❖ The *Application* section applies the math skill in a practical or real-life situation. You will learn how to put your knowledge into action by using manipulatives and calculators, and by working problems through with a partner or a group.

Each book ends with *Cumulative Reviews*. These reviews will help you determine if you have learned the skills in the previous lessons. The *Selected Answers* section at the end of each book lists answers to the odd-numbered exercises. Use the answers to check your work.

Working carefully through the exercises in this book will help you understand and appreciate math in your daily life. You'll also gain more confidence in your math skills.

ESTIMATING AND CALCULATING COSTS

Several friends held a book sale to collect money for their community center. Luis collected $14.86. Yuki collected $11.39. Al collected $12.52. Their goal was to donate $35. Did they reach their goal?

The friends estimate the total amount. To do this, they round each amount to the nearest dollar. Look at the first digit to the right of the decimal point. If it is 5 or more, they round up. If it is less than 5, they round down.

Round each number.   Add the rounded numbers.

$14.86 is rounded up to $15. $15
$11.39 is rounded down to $11. $11
$12.52 is rounded up to $13. $13
                                  $39

Luis, Yuki, and Al reached their goal.

To find the exact total, Luis adds each column, starting with the cents column.

$14.86
$11.39
+ $12.52
$38.77

Yuki uses a calculator. She clears the calculator of other numbers. Then she enters each amount followed by the ⊞ sign. After the last amount, she presses the ⊟ key.

Guided Practice

Reminder

Since Juan wants to be sure he has enough money, he rounds each amount up, even if the number to the right of the decimal is below 5.

1. Juan has $50 to spend at Music World. He wants to buy CDs that cost $12.99, $17.25, and $15.49. He estimates that sales tax will be about $4.

   Does he have enough money? __NO__

   Estimate: $13
             $18
             $16
           + $4
           _____

2. Odetta is buying cans of cat food. Each can costs $.89. About how much will 15 cans cost before tax?

 a. Round $.89 to the nearest dollar: _____

 b. Multiply the rounded amount by 15: $15.00

   The cat food will cost about $_____

Exercises

Estimate each answer.

3. Kit wants to buy paperback books that cost $5.25, $6.50, and $2.95. About how much will she spend on the books?

_____

4. The community center offers a trip to a theme park for $23.50 per person. Mike's family has $100 to spend. Can all 4 of them go?

_____

Find the exact answer.

5. The community center's driver buys a car battery costing $54 and windshield wipers costing $12. How much will he spend for these items?

_____

6. A group from the center goes to the movies. If Ling buys a ticket for $6.50, popcorn for $2.25, and juice for $1.75, how much will she spend?

_____

7. Gloria earns $5.25 an hour at the center. On Saturday she works 6 hours. How much will she earn?

_____

8. Bus tokens cost $1.35 each. How much will it cost Mrs. Diaz to buy 4 bus tokens for herself and her children?

_____

9. The center orders a tape player for $24.99, kitchen supplies for $14.79, and office supplies for $23.59. What is the cost?

_____

10. The center buys exercise equipment on the installment plan for $34.25 a month. How much of the bill will be paid after 36 months?

_____

Application

11. Write a few sentences explaining how you estimate a total when you have only a certain amount of money to spend.

_____

_____

_____

CALCULATING CHANGE

Lunch Menu

(Prices include sales tax)

Juice		Salads	
Apple	$1.50	Green	$1.85
Orange	$1.50	Fruit	$2.35
Veggie blend	$1.95	Cole slaw	$1.75
Hot Dishes		**Sandwiches**	
Burger	$2.65	Cheese	$2.25
Soup	$1.95	Turkey	$3.75
Burrito	$3.55	Deluxe	$4.75

Yoko buys apple juice, fruit salad, and a burrito. She pays with a $10 bill. How much change should she get?

You must solve this problem in two steps.

Reminder

When subtracting money amounts, write both numbers in dollars and cents.

Step 1 Get prices from the menu. Add to get the total.

$$\begin{array}{r} \$1.50 \\ 2.35 \\ + \ 3.55 \\ \hline \$7.40 \end{array}$$

Step 2 Subtract to find the change.

$$\begin{array}{r} \$10.00 \\ - \ 7.40 \\ \hline \$2.60 \end{array}$$

Yoko's change is $2.60.

Clay has $5. Can he get a hamburger and orange juice? Clay rounds each number up.

$2.65 rounds to $3.00; $1.50 rounds to $2.00.

$$\$3.00 + \$2.00 = \$5.00$$

Clay has enough money.

Reminder

When rounding to see whether you have enough money to buy several items, it helps to round every number up.

Guided Practice

1. Olga gets a deluxe sandwich, soup, a green salad, and veggie blend juice. How much change should she receive from $20?

   a. Find the total.

   $$\begin{array}{r} \$4.75 \\ 1.95 \\ 1.85 \\ + \ 1.95 \end{array}$$

   b. Subtract from $20.

   _____ Change

2. The restaurant owner has $50. She buys teabags for $23.99 and spices for $14.50. Can she also buy dried fruits costing $16.75?

    a. Estimate the total for the teabags and spices. $23.99 rounds to $24. $14.50 rounds up to $15. 24 + 15 = _____

    b. Subtract the estimate from $50. $50 – $ _____ = $ _____

    c. Can the owner buy the fruit? _____

Exercises

Find the correct change for each purchase.

3. A family's lunch bills come to $3.45, $6.70, $11.00, and $3.75. (Each bill includes tax.) The family pays with a $20 bill and a $10 bill. How much change will the family get?

_____

4. A tour group leader gives the cashier $50 for 7 breakfasts that cost $5.99 each, including tax. How much change will the group leader receive?

_____

5. The road runners group has a food budget of $450 for a day race. They order 37 box lunches for $6.85 each, including tax. How much money will be left?

_____

6. The restaurant owner buys a hammer for $18.94 and nails for $3.99. Sales tax on the purchase is $1.49. She pays with $30. How much change will she get?

_____

Estimate the answer.

7. Quentin's travel budget is $110. Bus fare is $42.50. He budgeted $36 for meals. Can he afford a blazer that costs $20.95?

_____

8. The coach has a budget of $200. She buys 32 lunches at a special group rate of $4.95. About how much money is left for other expenses?

_____

Application

COOPERATIVE
LEARNING

9. From the lunch menu, have each group choose a 3-item lunch for under $7.00. Compare your choices. List all possible 3-item lunches that cost less than $7.00.

_____

_____

_____

ESTIMATING AND CALCULATING BALANCES

Vocabulary

savings account: a bank account that earns interest

deposit: money put into a bank account

withdrawal: money taken out of an account

balance: the latest amount in an account; the result of deposits and/or withdrawals

Reminder

To compute using pencil and paper, align the numbers by place value before adding or subtracting. When adding money amounts, be sure to line up the decimal points.

Luz opened a bank **savings account** with a **deposit** of $125. Later she deposited $27. What is her new **balance**?

A deposit is money added to an account.

Opening balance: $125
Deposit: + 27
New balance: $152

Luz took $18 from the savings account to pay her cable TV bill. Money taken out of an account is called a **withdrawal**. To find the new balance, subtract.

Balance: $152
Withdrawal: − 18
New balance: $134

Luz's savings passbook looks like this:

Passbook number 30-246				Luz Rivera
Date	Deposit	Withdrawal	Interest	Balance
5/7/95	$125			$125
5/15/95	$27			$152
5/21/95		$18		$134

Withdrawals are in one column, deposits are in another column, and the balance after each transaction is in the last column.

Guided Practice

1. Kyang had $372.50 in his savings account. He deposited $114.23 today. What is his new balance?

   a. Write an addition in vertical form:

   Balance: _____

   Deposit: + _____

   b. _____

   New balance: _____

2. Keisha is thinking of buying a TV that costs $299.99. She has $563.48 saved in the bank. Estimate how much she will have left if she withdraws money for the TV.

a. Round each answer to the nearest hundred. $563.48 ⟶ _____

299.99 ⟶ _____

b. Subtract the rounded numbers.   Balance: _____

Exercises

Find the correct balance.

3. Mike's savings account had a balance of $635.14. Then he made a deposit of $197.38. What is his new balance?

_____

4. Eva had $1,285.16 in the bank. After 3 months, the bank added interest of $16.06. What is her new balance?

_____

5. Carmen had a savings account balance of $845.19. Then she withdrew $250. How much is left?

_____

6. Abu had $5,562.89 in a savings account. Then he took out $750. What is his new balance?

_____

Estimate.

7. Tyrell had $416.82 in the bank. Then he deposited $195.18. About how much does he have now?

_____

8. Inez had $953.04 in the bank. Then she took out $280.50. About how much is her new balance?

_____

Application

9. Work with a partner and act out bank transactions.

• Use 3 number cubes (dice) to generate the amount of deposits or withdrawals. Let one number cube represent the number in the hundreds place, another represent the number in the tens place, and another represent the number in the ones place. The person rolling the dice gets to decide which die represents which place.

• Make out 12 slips of paper that say either "deposit" or "withdrawal." Put these papers in a pile face down.

• Each partner starts with a balance of $1,000. For each turn, pick a slip of paper from the pile and roll the dice. That number becomes the amount of the deposit or the withdrawal. Add or subtract that number to determine the balance. The winner is the last person to have money left.

BALANCING CHECKING ACCOUNTS

Vocabulary

checking account: a bank account that allows customers to write checks that the bank will pay from the customer's deposits.

Reminder

Another way to find the new balance is to subtract the amount of each check individually.

Helena's **checking account** balance is $452.18. She plans to write checks for $23.50 and $14.75. What will her new balance be?

She must use two steps to find her new balance:

• First, add the check amounts to find the total withdrawal due to writing the checks.

• Then, subtract the total from the balance.

Add checks.

$$\begin{array}{r} \$23.50 \\ + \ 14.75 \\ \hline \$38.25 \end{array}$$

Subtract total from the balance.

$$\begin{array}{r} \$452.18 \\ - \ 38.25 \\ \hline \$413.93 \end{array}$$

The next day, Helena made a deposit of $150 and wrote a check for $45.60. Find her new balance:

Balance:	$413.93
Deposit:	+ 150.00
	$563.93
Check:	− 45.60
New balance:	$518.33

Helena records her balance, deposits, and checks in a balance book. The book shows the new balance after each transaction.

Date	Check	Withdrawal		Deposit		Balance	
8/3/95	64	$23	50			$452	18
	65	14	75			413	93
8/4/95				$150	00	563	93
	66	45	60			518	33

Guided Practice

1. Tru had $215.80 in his checking account. Then he deposited $45 and wrote a check for $116.20. What is his balance?

   a. Find the new balance after the deposit. $215.80

   $+ 45.00$

b. Find the new balance after the check.   − 116.20 = _____

2. Elena had $623.85 in her account. Then she wrote checks for $38.15, $21.58, and $14.82. About how much is left?

    a. Round each amount to the nearest $10. $38.15 ⟶ _____

                                           21.58 ⟶ _____

                                           14.82 ⟶ _____

    b. Add to estimate the withdrawals.   _____

    c. Round the balance to the nearest $10. $623.85 ⟶ _____

    d. Subtract the estimated total you got in b.   − _____

Exercises

3. Jamal had $709.73 in his checking account. Then he wrote a check for $25 and one for $123.50. What is his new balance?

_____

4. Chun Li had $517 in her checking account. Then she deposited $50 and wrote a check for $75.16. What is her new balance?

_____

 5. Complete Sandra's checking account book by finding the balance for September 26.

Date	Check	Withdrawal	Deposit	Balance
9/1				$4,623.82
9/8			$2,831.75	
9/9	89	$167.00		
9/14	90	$3,090.50		
9/17			$35.63	
9/26		$86.80		_____

Estimate.

6. Laura had $815.93 in her checking account. Then she wrote checks for $64.52, $38.90, $12.07 and $52.95. About how much is left in her account? _____

Application

7. Write a list of instructions for finding the balance in a checking account when it includes several deposits and withdrawals. In what order do you think it is best to enter the transactions? Why?

_____

CHANGING FRACTIONS TO DECIMALS

Vocabulary

numerator: the top part of a fraction; it tells how many pieces are in the part

denominator: the bottom part of a fraction; it tells the number of equal pieces that are in the whole

Reminder

In a decimal number, each place to the right of the decimal point has a place value name.

tenths	hundredths	thousandths
. 3		
. 0	5	
. 0	6	7

These numbers are read:
"3 tenths"
"5 hundredths"
"67 thousandths"

Julia needs $\frac{3}{4}$ pound of salami to make sandwiches. The store uses a decimal scale that shows tenths and hundredths of a pound. Does Julia have enough salami if the scale reads 0.76?

A fraction is a way to express a number that shows part of a whole. Each rectangle below is divided into equal pieces. Some of those pieces are shaded. The fraction next to each rectangle shows what part the shaded section is of the whole rectangle.

 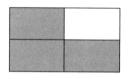

A decimal is another way to express a number that is part of a whole. To change a fraction to a decimal, divide the numerator by the denominator.

For example, Julia wants to change $\frac{3}{4}$ to a decimal.

$$4\overline{)3.00}^{\,0.75} \qquad \frac{3}{4} = 0.75 \text{ as a decimal.}$$

Since the scale shows 0.76, Julia has enough salami.

Some fractions, such as $\frac{1}{4}$, $\frac{3}{5}$, and $\frac{1}{2}$, can be easily converted into decimals. Other fractions, such as $\frac{1}{3}$ or $\frac{3}{8}$, do not divide evenly. Use a calculator to convert $\frac{1}{3}$ into a decimal. What do you notice?

Input 1 ⊡ 3

The display reads 0.33333333.

If you find yourself working with such a fraction, round your decimal to the hundredths place.

$\frac{1}{3}$ is approximately equal to 0.33

Guided Practice

1. Julia also bought some packages of chicken. They weigh $2\frac{1}{2}$ pounds, $3\frac{1}{4}$ pounds, and $4\frac{5}{8}$ pounds. To estimate how much she has in all, round the weights.

For fractions that are less than $\frac{1}{2}$, round down.

$$3\frac{1}{4} \longrightarrow 3$$

For fractions that are $\frac{1}{2}$ or greater, round up.

$$2\frac{1}{2} \longrightarrow 3 \quad \text{and} \quad 4\frac{5}{8} \longrightarrow 5$$

Add the rounded amounts: $3 + 3 + 5 = 11$. Julia bought about 11 pounds of chicken.

Exercises

Write each fraction as a decimal.

2. $\frac{1}{4} =$ _____

3. $\frac{3}{10} =$ _____

4. $\frac{4}{5} =$ _____

5. $\frac{3}{8} =$ _____

6. A piece of copper wire is $7\frac{1}{8}$ meters long. Write this measure as a decimal.

_____

7. Jetta gets paid $9 per hour. She worked for $12\frac{3}{4}$ hours last weekend. To find her earnings on a calculator, she must change $12\frac{3}{4}$ to a decimal. Write the hours using decimals.

_____

Estimate each answer.

8. A bakery storeroom had $23\frac{3}{4}$ lb of sugar this morning. The bakers used $6\frac{1}{2}$ lb of sugar today. About how much is left?

_____

9. A grocery bag contains $7\frac{1}{2}$ lb of rice, 5 lb of potatoes, and $4\frac{3}{4}$ lb. of onions. About how heavy is the bag?

_____

Application

10. Decimals are a way to divide a whole into 10 parts, 100 parts, or 1,000 parts. How does knowing this help you understand why the fractions $\frac{1}{2}$, $\frac{3}{5}$, or $\frac{1}{4}$ can easily be converted into decimals while $\frac{1}{3}$ or $\frac{1}{6}$ cannot?

_____

_____

SOLVING PROBLEMS WITH FRACTIONS

Problem 1

Mr. Hidalgo sells wire in his hardware store. Today, he began with a coil of 50 yards of wire. One customer bought $4\frac{1}{2}$ yards. Another customer bought $5\frac{1}{4}$ yards. How much wire is left on the coil?

To find out how much wire is left, add the amounts of wire sold. First give the fractions the same denominator.

$$4\frac{1}{2} \longrightarrow 4\frac{2}{4}$$
$$+\ 5\frac{1}{4} \longrightarrow 5\frac{1}{4}$$
$$\overline{\qquad\qquad 9\frac{3}{4} \text{ yards sold}}$$

Then subtract the total from 50 yards.

$$50 \longrightarrow 49\frac{4}{4}$$
$$-\ 9\frac{3}{4} \longrightarrow -\ 9\frac{3}{4}$$
$$\overline{\qquad\qquad 40\frac{1}{4} \text{ yards left}}$$

Problem 2

Mr. Hidalgo also sells pine bark mulch at $2 per cubic foot. Tia bought $16\frac{1}{2}$ cubic feet on Monday and $10\frac{3}{4}$ cubic feet on Tuesday. How much did she spend on mulch?

First add.

$$16\frac{1}{2} \longrightarrow 16\frac{2}{4}$$
$$+\ 10\frac{3}{4} \longrightarrow 10\frac{3}{4}$$
$$\overline{\qquad\qquad 26\frac{5}{4} = 27\frac{1}{4}}$$

Then multiply. Since you are working with money, change the fraction to a decimal.

$$27\frac{1}{4} \longrightarrow 27.25$$
$$\underline{\times\ 2}$$
$$54.50$$

Tia spent $54.50 on mulch.

1. Elinor has $\frac{7}{8}$ yard of ribbon. She cut pieces that measured $\frac{1}{4}$ yard and $\frac{1}{8}$ yard. How much ribbon is left?

   a. Change $\frac{1}{4}$ into eighths.

   $$\frac{1}{4} = \frac{2}{8} \rightarrow$$

   b. Add the cut lengths. _____

   $$+ \quad \frac{1}{8}$$

   Total: _____

   c. Subtract the total from $\frac{7}{8}$.

   $$\frac{7}{8}$$

   $$-$$

   _____

   _____ yards left

Solve.

2. Ali cut two pieces from a 9-foot length of pipe. One piece was $2\frac{1}{2}$ feet long. The other was $\frac{7}{8}$ foot long. How much pipe is left?

   _____

3. For a woodworking class, Ella has $2\frac{1}{2}$ hours to complete a three-part test. The first part took $\frac{1}{4}$ hour. The next part took $1\frac{1}{2}$ hours. How much time is left?

   _____

Estimate the answer.

4. An oil company's tank held 600 gallons of oil. It made deliveries of $238\frac{1}{2}$ gallons and $189\frac{7}{8}$ gallons. About how many gallons are left?

   _____

5. Felipe earns $7.25 per hour. Last week he worked 7 hours, $7\frac{1}{2}$ hours, $8\frac{1}{4}$ hours, $6\frac{1}{2}$ hours, and 8 hours. About how much did he earn?

   _____

6. A garden supply store sells pine bark nuggets in bags that hold $3\frac{1}{2}$ cubic feet each and cost $4.38. It also sells a bag that holds $5\frac{1}{2}$ cubic feet of the nuggets and costs $5.75. Which is the better buy? Explain how you know your answer is correct.

   _____

FINDING SALES TAX AND DISCOUNT

Vocabulary

percent: per hundred—for example, 1% is $\frac{1}{100}$.

discount: a reduction in price, often figured as a percentage.

sales tax: a percentage of an item's price; sales tax goes to the local or state government.

base: the original price of an item

rate: the percent of a discount or a tax

Reminder

To multiply decimals, give the product the same number of decimal places as the combined number of decimal places in both multiplied numbers.

.26	2 decimal places
× .002	3 decimal places
.00052	5 decimal places

Reminder

To round to the nearest cent, look at the digit in the thousandths place. Round up if the digit is 5 or greater. Round down if it is less than 5.

Many stores offer reduced prices from time to time. A **discount** is the amount the store will take off from the regular price. Often, a discount is given as a **percent**.

Percent means per hundred. A discount of 30% means that for every $1 of the price, the store will take off $0.30.

To find the amount of a discount, multiply the base by the rate. The **base** is the original price. The **rate** is the percent.

- Change the rate from a percent to a decimal or fraction.

- Multiply the base by this decimal or fraction.

Problem 1

A coat with a regular price of $90 is on sale for 35% off. How much money is being taken off the regular price?

$$35\% = \frac{35}{100} = 0.35$$

(Notice that you have moved the decimal point two places to the left to convert 35% to 0.35.)

$$
\begin{array}{r}
\$90 \\
\times\ 0.35 \\
\hline
450 \\
270 \\
\hline
\$31.50
\end{array}
$$
The discount is $31.50.

Percents are also used to find the amount of sales tax.

Problem 2

In Millwood the sales tax is 5%. How much sales tax will José owe if he buys $56.25 worth of items?

a. Change 5% to a decimal. 5% = 0.05

b. Multiply.

c. The product will have 4 decimal places.

$$
\begin{array}{r}
\$56.25 \\
\times\ 0.05 \\
\hline
2.8125
\end{array}
$$

d. Round to the nearest cent: $2.81 is the sales tax.

Guided Practice

1. A $15 CD has a 12% discount. Find the amount of the discount.

   a. Change 12% to a decimal. 12% = _____

   b. Multiply. $15   (the regular price)

   ×_____   (the discount as a decimal)

   _____   (the product)

   The discount is $ _____

Exercises

FILLMORE'S STOREWIDE SALE!

40% discount on CD players   16% discount on sneakers
20% discount on jeans   25% discount on coats

Use the sales announcement to solve problems 2–5.
Give the discount for each of the following items:

2. a CD player costing $125

3. jeans costing $29.99

4. a coat costing $98

5. sneakers costing $49

Estimate by rounding the price.

6. The sales tax rate is $2\frac{1}{2}$% (0.025 as a decimal). About how much tax will Jenny pay on a video game that costs $52.99?

7. Drake is buying a used car for $1,725. The sales tax rate is 7%. About how much sales tax will Drake pay on the car?

Application

COOPERATIVE
LEARNING

Work with a small group. Solve 8–11. Then discuss 12 and 13..

8. 2% of $10,000 _____

9. 2% of $4 _____

10. 60% of $500 _____

11. 60% of $8 _____

12. Is it ever worth going out of your way for a discount of less than 5%?

13. Does a discount of 60% mean that you will pay less than half the original price?

CALCULATING THE FINAL COST

Vocabulary

sale price: the price after the discount has been subtracted

Reminder

The amount of the discount is the amount that is subtracted from the original price.

Reminder

A sales tax is an amount added to the cost.

Problem 1

Latoya wants to buy a portable cassette player. The regular price is $42. It is on sale for 20% off. What is the sale price?

Step 1: Multiply to find the discount.

$$
\begin{array}{rr}
\text{regular price} \longrightarrow & \$42 \\
\text{discount rate} \longrightarrow & \times\ 0.20 \\
\hline
\text{discount} \longrightarrow & \$8.40
\end{array}
$$

Step 2: Subtract to find the sale price.

$$
\begin{array}{rr}
\text{regular price} \longrightarrow & \$42.00 \\
\text{discount} \longrightarrow & -\ 8.40 \\
\hline
\text{sale price} \longrightarrow & \$33.60
\end{array}
$$

Problem 2

The sales tax where Latoya lives is $3\frac{1}{4}\%$. Find the total price she will pay for the cassette player.

Sales tax is added to the price of an item.

Step 1: Multiply to find the sales tax.

$$
\begin{array}{rr}
\text{price} \longrightarrow & \$33.60 \\
\text{tax rate} \longrightarrow & \times\ 0.0325 \\
\hline
\text{sales tax} \longrightarrow & 1.09200
\end{array}
$$
rounded: $1.09

Step 2: Add to find the total price.

$$
\begin{array}{rr}
\text{price} \longrightarrow & \$33.60 \\
\text{sales tax} \longrightarrow & +\ 1.09 \\
\hline
\text{total price} \longrightarrow & \$34.69
\end{array}
$$

Guided Practice

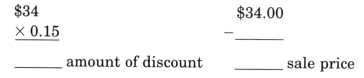

1. Find the sale price of a denim shirt with a regular price of $34. The discount is 15%.

   a. Find the discount.   **b.** Find the sale price.

   $34
   × 0.15
   _____

   _____ amount of discount $34.00
   − _____

   _____ sale price

2. Find the total price of an audiocassette with a price of $12.75 and a sales tax of 4%.

a. Find the amount of tax.

$12.75
$\times\ 0.04$

_____ amount of tax

b. Find the total price.

$12.75
+_____

_____ total price

Solve.

3. Keith has a coupon for 25% off a plane ticket that normally costs $179. What is the price that Keith will pay?

_____

4. The Wu family's bill at the restaurant is for $24.50. They have a discount coupon for 15%. How much will they pay before sales tax?

_____

5. Hector bought a raincoat at 20% off. The regular price is $35.50. What is the sale price?

_____

6. Mrs. Khan bought a washing machine for $250. The sales tax is 4%. What is her total price?

_____

Estimate by rounding the price.

7. Find the sale price of a TV after a 20% discount. The regular price is $382.14.

_____

8. Find the sale price of a coat that lists for $125 if it is on sale for 40% off.

_____

Application

9. Which is the better buy: a pair of shoes that originally cost $49 but has been reduced by 20%, or a pair of shoes that originally cost $35 but that has been reduced by 15%? Give the answer. Then explain how a calculator can help you with comparison shopping.

_____

_____

_____

FINDING PERCENTS

Assam is visiting his aunt. He bought a shirt costing $15 and paid $0.45 in sales tax. What is the sales tax rate in his aunt's town?

To find the rate as a percent, follow these steps:

- Divide the amount of tax by the base (the item's price).

- Change the result from a decimal to a percent.

Assam paid $0.45 in sales tax. This is the amount. The shirt cost $15. This is the base.

Notice that you are dividing the *smaller* number by the *larger* number. So, your answer will always be less than 1.

$$15\overline{)0.45} = 0.03$$

Change 0.03 to a percent by moving the decimal point two places to the right.

$$0.\underset{\smile}{03} = 3\%$$

The sales tax rate is 3%.

Reminder

To multiply by a percent, rewrite the percent as a decimal or a fraction.

Reminder

If your calculator has a percent key, you can convert your decimal answer to a percent with the calculator. Read the instruction booklet to find out in what order you need to press the keys to convert a decimal to a percent.

Guided Practice

1. Chelsea bought a book that usually costs $25 for $5 less. What percent discount did she get on the book?

  a. Divide.

$$25\overline{)5.00}$$

  b. Change the decimal result to a percent.

_____ = _____%

2. Bert paid $16.25 less for a pair of jeans with a regular price of $25.99. What is the percent discount, to the nearest percent?

  a. Divide on a calculator:

16.25 ÷ 25.99 = _____

  b. Round the display to the nearest whole percent:

_____

Reminder

To round to a given place, look at the digit to the right of the rounding place.
5 or more—round up;
less than 5—round down

Exercises

Solve.

3. The sales tax on a $24 baseball game ticket is $1.20. Find the sales tax percent.

_____

4. A CD that costs $15 is on sale for $3.75 off. What is the percent of the discount?

_____

5. A video game that costs $60 is on sale for $15 off. What is the percent of the discount?

_____

6. Otis bought a plant for $8 and paid $0.20 sales tax. What is the sales tax rate as a percent?

_____

7. At Pen Works, 12 out of 50 employees are part-time workers. What percent of the workers are part-time workers?

_____

8. Lei-Lei makes $210 a week now. Soon she will get a raise of $14.70 a week. What percent of her current salary is her raise?

_____

Round to the nearest whole percent.

9. Dave bought software costing $54.99. He received a discount of $10 off that price. What is the percent of the discount?

_____

10. Lucy paid $380 less for a refrigerator originally priced at $700. What percent discount did she get?

_____

Application

11. Write a paragraph explaining how to find the percent of the sale if you know the amount of the discount and the original price.

_____

_____

_____

_____

_____

_____

SOLVING PROBLEMS ABOUT PERCENT

Denise paid $13 for a T-shirt that cost $12.50 before tax. What was the percent of the sales tax?

First subtract to find the amount of the tax.

$$\$13.00 \longleftarrow Price \ including \ tax$$
$$\underline{- \ 12.50} \longleftarrow Price$$
$$\$0.50 \longleftarrow Amount \ of \ sales \ tax \ paid$$
$$on \ \$12.50$$

Then divide to find the percent rate of the tax.

- Divide the amount, $.50 or 0.5, by the base, 12.50 or 12.5. Since you can't divide by a decimal, you must move the decimal point in 12.5 to make a whole number. Then you must move the decimal point in 0.5 the *same number of places*.

$$12.5\overline{)0.5} \longrightarrow 125\overline{)5.00}^{.04}$$
$$\underline{- \ 5 \ 00}$$

- Change the result, 0.04, to a percent. $0.04 \longrightarrow 4\%$

The sales tax is 4%.

Guided Practice

1. Felix bought a videotape for $16.80. The regular price is $24. What percent discount did he get?

   a. Find the amount of the discount:

   $$\$24.00$$
   $$\underline{- \ 16.80}$$

   _____ ⟵ Amount of discount

   b. Divide the amount of the discount by the base, 24.

   $24\overline{)}$

   c. Change the result from part b to a percent by moving the decimal point two places to the right:
   _____ ⟶ _____ %

2. Tina paid $15.05 for a CD that costs $14. What is the sales tax percent?

   a. Use a calculator. Find the amount of the tax.

   $$\$15.05 - 14.00 = _____ \longleftarrow Amount \ of \ tax$$

b. Divide the amount of the tax by the base, 14.

_____ ÷ 14 = _____

c. Change the result to a percent: _____ $\longrightarrow$ _____ %

Exercises

Solve. Round answers to the nearest tenth of a percent.

3. Abby bought a $36 radio. Including tax, the price came to $37.80. What is the sales tax percent?

_____

4. Linda bought a hair dryer for $10. The regular price was $14. What percent discount did Linda get?

_____

5. Javier paid $23.48 including tax for a book. The price of the book is $22.80. What is the sales tax percent?

_____

6. Bill has a coupon for an airplane ticket that usually costs $450. Bill paid only $375. What percent discount did he get?

_____

7. Teresa bought a skirt that usually costs $35. She paid only $24.50. What percent discount did she get?

_____

8. Farah paid $56 for a tool kit that lists for $80. What percent discount did she get on the kit?

_____

9. Ellen bought sneakers for $34.20. The price before tax was $32.99. What percent sales tax did she pay?

_____

10. Leroy bought dinner for his family for $24. He paid the cashier $24.96 to cover tax. What percent sales tax did he pay?

_____

Application

COOPERATIVE LEARNING

11. Work in a small group. Find ads in newspapers and/or magazines that state a regular price and a sale price. Determine the percent of the discount offered in each. Which of the ads you have found offers the best sale?

_____

_____

_____

FINDING THE BASE

Miguel made 9 of his free throw attempts during the championship game. This was 75% of his free throw attempts. How many free throws did he attempt?

In this problem, you know the percent, 75%, and the amount of the percent, 9. You want to find the base, which is the number of shots attempted in all.

To find the base, divide the amount of the percent by the percent written as a decimal.

- Change 75% to a decimal by moving the decimal point two places to the left.

$$75\% \longrightarrow 0.75$$

- Divide 9 by 0.75.

$$
0.75\overline{)9} \longrightarrow
\begin{array}{r}
12 \\
75\overline{)900} \\
\underline{750} \\
150 \\
\underline{150} \\
\end{array}
$$

Miguel attempted 12 shots in all.

Reminder

It is easier to divide by a whole number than by a decimal. Change the decimal to a whole number by moving the decimal point to the right. Then move the decimal point in the dividend the same number of places to the right.

Guided Practice

1. In a factory, 20 flashlights were found to be defective one day. This is 1% of the flashlights produced that day. How many were produced?

   a. Change 1% to a decimal: _____

   b. Divide 20 by the answer to part a.

   _____ $\overline{)20}$

   Remember to move the decimal points to the right.

2. Isabel puts $25 in a savings account every week. This is 5% of her weekly salary. What is her weekly salary?

   a. Change 5% to a decimal: _____

   b. Divide 25 by the answer to part a.

   _____ $\overline{)25}$

   Remember to move the decimal points.

Solve. Round to the nearest whole number or cent.

3. Darlene made 16 field goals, which was 80% of her field goal attempts. How many field goals did she attempt?

_____

4. Joe hit the ball 24 times last week. This was 30% of his at-bats. How many at-bats did he have last week?

_____

5. Mikiko got a 24% discount on a movie ticket. This saved her $1.25. What was the regular price of the ticket?

_____

6. Tara bought a coat and paid $15 less than the regular price. This discount was 5% of the regular price. What was the regular price?

_____

7. Today 21 employees of Perfect Plastics called in sick. This is 2% of the total number of employees. How many people work at Perfect Plastics?

_____

8. Tawana answered 85% of the questions on a test correctly. She answered 34 questions correctly. How many questions were on the test?

_____

9. A glass of skim milk contains 8.8 mg of calcium. This is 1.1% of the recommended daily allowance (RDA) for a child. What is the RDA of calcium for a child?

_____

10. A banana contains 12 mg of vitamin C. This is 20% of the RDA of vitamin C for an adult. What is the RDA of vitamin C for an adult?

_____

Application

COOPERATIVE LEARNING

11. Make up two problems in which a percent and the amount of the percent are given and the base must be found. Exchange problems with a partner. Evaluate whether your partner's problems give the necessary information. Then solve your partner's problems.

_____

_____

_____

_____

_____

SOLVING PERCENT PROBLEMS ABOUT BASE

The quarterback threw several passes during the game. Of those passes, 5 were completed in the first quarter, 6 were completed in the second quarter, 3 were completed in the third quarter, and 4 were completed in the fourth quarter. Of the passes the quarterback attempted, 40% were completed. How many passes did the quarterback attempt during the game?

First, find the total number of passes that were completed.

$$5 + 6 + 3 + 4 = 18 \text{ passes}$$

You know the number of passes completed and the percent of passes completed. You are looking for the base, the total number of passes thrown.

$$0.40\overline{)18.00} \longrightarrow \begin{array}{r} 45 \\ 40\overline{)1800} \\ \underline{160} \\ 200 \\ \underline{200} \end{array}$$

18 is 40% of 45.

45 passes were thrown.

Guided Practice

1. During the game, 12 points were scored on field goals, which are worth 3 points each. The kicker made 80% of his field goal attempts. How many field goals did he attempt?

   a. First, find the number of field goals that were successful. Since 12 points were scored and field goals earn 3 points each, divide 12 by 3.

   $12 \div 3 =$ _____ field goals made

   b. Now you know the number of field goals made (4) and the percent of the total attempted (80%). You need to find the base, the number of field goals attempted. Divide 4 by the percent rate as a decimal.

   _____$\overline{)}$_____

Solve.

2. On the softball team, Eva had 8 more at-bats last week than Mary did. Mary had 15 hits, which was 25% of her at-bats. How many at-bats did Eva have?

_____

3. Akim bought a portable CD player for $21 off the regular price. This was a discount of 15%. What was the sale price of the CD player?

_____

4. In a basketball game, Duc Lo made 3 of the 3-point shots he attempted. This number was 60% of all the 3-pointers he attempted. If he had scored all his three-pointers, how many points would he have scored?

_____

5. Wanda finished 8 of the potholders she is making for the craft fair. This is 40% of the potholders she plans to make. She can sell potholders for $4.50 each. How much will she earn if she sells all the potholders she plans to make?

 _____

6. Dahlia bought a word processor for $25 off the regular price. This was a 5% discount. What was the sale price of the word processor?

_____

7. Last year Manuel saved 8% of his salary. The amount he saved was $2288. A year has 52 weeks. How much does he make a week?

 _____

8. There are a few weeks left of the fire department's fundraiser. So far, $90,000 has been raised. This is 60% of the goal amount. How much more must be raised to meet the goal?

_____

9. Lida is conducting a test of a computer system. The screen tells her that the test is 30% complete. So far the test has taken 45 minutes. How much longer will the test take to complete?

_____

Application

10. Choose one of the problems on this page. Write directions for solving the problem. Explain why each step is needed.

_____

_____

SOLVING EQUATIONS

Paul has saved $257. He wants to go on a vacation that will cost $450. How much more money does he need to save?

One way to solve a problem is to let a letter stand for the unknown number. Because this letter could stand for any number, it is called a **variable**.

Then use the facts in the problem to write an **equation**. An equation is a math sentence that shows equality between two quantities. Everything stated on one side of the equal sign equals everything stated on the other side.

In Paul's problem, the unknown is the amount of money he still needs to save for the vacation.

Let m represent the amount of money he needs.

$257 + m = 450$ is an equation based on the facts in the problem.

To find what number added to 257 gives the sum 450, subtract 257 from 450.

$$m = 450 - 257$$
$$m = 193$$

Paul needs to save $193 more for his vacation.

Here is another example.

Gina collects baseball cards. She keeps them in a looseleaf binder, in special plastic pages. The pages cost $.15 each. How many pages can she buy with $2.50?

Let p represent the number of pages she can buy.

An equation based on the problem is $0.15 \times p = 2.50$.

To find out what number multiplied by 0.15 equals 2.50, divide 2.50 by .15. On a calculator, the result will read 16.66666667. Gina could not buy more than 16 pages.

To check your answer, look back at the problem. If Gina bought 16 pages, she would pay $.15 × 16 for them.

$$\$.15 \times 16 = \$2.40$$

Vocabulary

variable: a symbol (usually a letter) that can stand for a number

equation: a math sentence that shows equality between two quantities

Reminder

To keep things equal in an equation, whatever you do on one side of the equal sign must be done on the other side. If you remove 2 from one side of the equation, you have to remove 2 from the other side also.

$n + 2 = 4$
$n + 2 - 2 = 4 - 2$
$n = 2$

Reminder

Each operation has an opposite operation. Adding 2 is the opposite of subtracting 2. Dividing by 7 is the opposite of multiplying by 7.

Guided Practice

1. Antoine has 6 cousins. He gave each one 25 stamps from his collection. How many stamps did he give away?

   a. Choose an equation for this problem. Let s represent the total number of stamps given away.

   A. $s - 6 = 25$ **B.** $s \div 6 = 25$

   C. $s = 25 \div 6$ **D.** $s = 25 - 6$

   b. Solve the equation. Total number of stamps given away:

   _____

Exercises

Choose an equation for this problem. Then solve.

2. Jaconda spent $6.50 of her allowance at the movies. She had $5.50 left. How much is her allowance?

   Let a represent her allowance.

   a. $a + 6.50 = 5.50$ **b.** $6.50 - a = 5.50$ **c.** $a - 6.50 = 5.50$

   Total allowance: _____

Write an equation for this problem. Then solve.

3. Elizabeth filled 12 cartons with canned food for the food drive. Each carton contained 24 cans. How many cans did she pack?

   Let c represent the number of cans she packed.

   Equation: _____

   Number of cans in all: _____

Application

COOPERATIVE
LEARNING

4. Work with a small group. Think of a business or store you have visited recently. Make up a problem about the goods or services provided by that business. Choose a variable to represent the unknown number in your problem. After each person has written a problem, work as a group to write equations and solve the problems.

USING EQUATIONS IN TWO-STEP PROBLEMS

Reminder

To use a formula, substitute the values you are given. Then do the operations.

Reminder

To write an equation for a problem, start by choosing a letter to represent the number you need to find.

Jeff has a can of outdoor paint that can only be used if the air temperature is 55°F or above. Jeff's outdoor thermometer states that the air temperature is 10°C. Can Jeff use the paint at that temperature?

The formula for changing Celsius temperature to Fahrenheit temperature is:

$$F = \frac{9}{5} C + 32$$

First, substitute 10° for C in the formula. Instead of multiplying 9 × 10, you can cancel the denominator of the fraction because 10 is a multiple of 5.

$$F = \frac{9}{\cancel{5}} \times \cancel{10}^2 + 32$$
$$F = 9 \times 2 + 32$$
$$F = 18 + 32$$
$$F = 50$$

The air temperature is 50°F.

Next, compare this temperature with 55°F. Since it is less than 55°F, the paint cannot be used at that temperature.

Julia has filled 100 grapefruit crates. Each crate holds 40 grapefruits. Each grapefruit will sell for $.50. How much will Julia receive for selling all the grapefruits?

First, find out how many grapefruits were packed in all.

Let g represent the total number of grapefruits.

Then the equation is $g \div 40 = 100$.

To find g, multiply 100 by 40.

$$g = 100 \times 40 = 4,000$$

Next, find the cost of 4,000 grapefruits at $.50 each.

$$4,000 \times \$.50 = \$2,000$$

Guided Practice

1. Rosa bought a CD for $16 and some cassettes for $5 each. She spent $31 in all. How many cassettes did she buy?

a. Find c, the total she spent on cassettes. $16 + c = 31$

$c =$ _____

b. Find the number of cassettes she bought for $5 each. (Decide whether you must add, subtract, multiply, or divide.)

_____

Solve.

2. Tim received $7.75 change from a $20 bill after buying 7 pens. How much did each pen cost, including tax?

3. Luz bought 5 notebooks and got $6.25 change back from $10. How much did each notebook cost, including tax?

4. Lamark's car gets 22 miles per gallon of gasoline. He must make a 250-mile trip. Gasoline costs $1.49 per gallon. How much will gasoline for the trip cost?

5. Marina and her sister are saving for a $420 color TV. Each sister will pay half the cost. Marina has $75 saved. How much more must she save for her share of the cost?

6. Midori's refrigerator keeps a constant temperature of 40°F. The outdoor thermometer shows a temperature of 20°C. Which is lower?

7. Felipe attempted 50 field goals during a game. He failed to make 27 of them. Each goal he made earned 2 points. How many points did he earn from his successful goals?

Application

COOPERATIVE

LEARNING

8. Work with a group. Choose one problem from the Exercises (except for Exercise 4) and work together to demonstrate and explain how you would use a calculator to find the answer. Did you all use the same method? Did anyone come up with a useful shortcut?

_____

_____

_____

WRITING A SITUATION FOR AN EQUATION

Reminder

Adding is putting groups together.
Subtracting is taking away or comparing or seeing how many more you need.
Multiplying is repeated addition.
Dividing is finding how many groups of a certain size you can make from the total or finding the size of a certain number of equal groups.

Write a problem that can be solved by the equation

$$x + 45 = 70$$

One way to see what this equation means is to model it with some paper clips. This diagram shows that we are looking for the number that, when added to 45, gives a sum of 70.

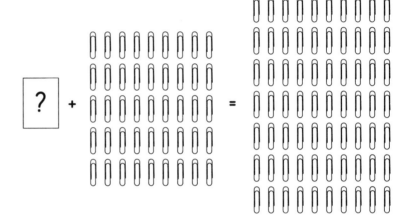

Here are three problems that would match this equation.

1. The window is 45 inches wide. The total width of the window and the shutters is 70 inches. What is the width of the shutters?

2. Steve and Noah put their money together to buy a canoe that costs $70. Steve paid $45. How much did Noah pay?

3. Claire waited 70 minutes on line to get tickets to a rock concert. That was 45 minutes more than Lashondra waited. How long did Lashondra wait?

The equation $15 - y = 3$ can be modeled with paper clips also.

Start with 15. How many must you take away so that you only have 3 left?

Here is a problem for this equation:

Alicia went to a book fair. She had $15 to spend. When she left the fair, she had $3 left. How much did she spend?

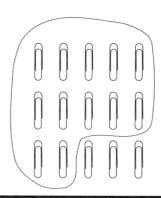

Guided Practice

Complete the problem for each equation.

1. Equation: $5 \times n = 105$
Jill has a pocket full of nickels. The total value is $1.05.

_____

_____

2. Equation: $z \div 8 = 4$
Darryl poured milk into 8-ounce glasses. He was able to fill 4 glasses.

_____

_____

Exercises

Write a problem for each equation. You may use the situation that is given, but you don't have to.

3. $a + 15,000 = 40,000$ (Two bank accounts add up to $40,000.)

_____

_____

4. $b - 6 = 21$ (After 6 days, there are 21 days left.)

_____

_____

Application

COOPERATIVE
LEARNING

5. Work with a partner. Each partner writes three equations. Then exchange papers. Write at least two different problems for each of your partner's equations. Then work together to read and discuss all the problems you have written. Do the problems fit the equations?

Reminder

There are two ways to show multiplication if a variable is involved. One way is to show the multiplication sign. The other is to write the number next to the variable.

$$2 \times n \quad \text{or} \quad 2n$$

WRITING A PROBLEM FOR A TWO-STEP EQUATION

Write a problem that can be solved by the equation

$$2n + 40 = 70$$

You already know that to solve an equation, you need to add, subtract, multiply, or divide. To solve this equation, you must perform *two* operations. You know this because you see a plus sign and the expression $2n$, which means "2 times n." So the equation means the following:

- Begin with an unknown value.
- Double it, or multiply by 2.
- Next, add 40.
- The result is 70.

Here are two problems for this equation.

1. Graciela spent $70 at the housewares store. She bought a stool for $40. The rest she spent on 2 lamps. Both lamps cost the same amount. How much did each lamp cost?

2. Greg spent 70 minutes doing laundry. He spent 40 minutes running the washing machine and the remainder of the time running the dryer. He did 2 loads in the dryer. How long did each load take to run?

The equation $16 - 3y = 4$ must also be solved in two steps.

- Begin with an unknown value and multiply it by 3.
- Next, subtract it from 16.

The result is 4.

Here is a problem for this equation:

Hector earned $16. He bought 3 T-shirts. At the end of the day, he had $4 left. How much did each T-shirt cost?

Complete the problem for each equation.

1. Equation: $5n + 25 = 130$
Jill has sold 130 raffle tickets. She sold 5 books of tickets and 25 loose tickets.

_____

2. Equation: $r - 7 + 5 = 13$
At a meeting, 7 people left early, and 5 arrived late. By the end of the meeting there were 13 people in the room.

_____

Exercises

Write a problem for each equation. You may use the situation that is given, but you don't have to.

3. $2a + 500 = 800$ (A three-plex movie house has 800 seats in all.)

_____

_____

4. $4g + 10 = 38$ (In the post office, 4 identical packages are waiting to be mailed, along with one that weighs 10 ounces.)

_____

_____

Application

5. Choose a problem from the Exercises. Explain what you would do to solve the equation for that problem.

_____

_____

USING PROPORTIONS

Vocabulary

ratio: a comparison of two numbers

proportion: a statement that two ratios are equal

The stationery store is selling pencils at $.25 for 3. A sign on the counter also tells the price for 6, 9 and 12 pencils.

The cost of the pencils, $.25 for 3, is an example of a **ratio**. A ratio is a comparison of two numbers. Each of the other prices on the chart are the same ratio.

$$\frac{\$.25}{3} = \frac{\$.50}{6} = \frac{\$.75}{9} = \frac{\$1.00}{12}$$

A statement that two ratios are equal is called a **proportion**. You can tell if two ratios form a proportion by comparing their cross-products. Do this by multiplying the numerator (top number) of one ratio by the denominator (bottom number) of the other.

$$\frac{0.25}{3} \times \frac{0.50}{6}$$

$$6 \times 0.25 = 3 \times 0.50$$

$$1.50 = 1.50$$

Reminder

In the word elephant, the ratio of vowels to consonants is 3 to 5. This can be written as 3:5 or $\frac{3}{5}$.

Reminder

You can use a letter to stand for a number you are looking for.

Reminder

Whatever you do on one side of an equation, you have to do on the other side. To solve an equation like $4 \times y = 20$, you know that the value of each side is 4 y's. If you need to find the value of 1 y, divide both sides by 4.

$$4y = 20 \longrightarrow y = \frac{20}{4}$$

$$y = 5$$

Dawanna has $3.50. How many pencils can she buy?

Solve this problem by writing a proportion equation. Let p stand for the number of pencils she can buy for $3.50.

Then, $$\frac{.025}{3} = \frac{3.50}{p}$$

Use the cross-products rule:

$$0.25 \times p = 3 \times 3.50$$

$$0.25 \times p = 10.50$$

$$p = \frac{10.50}{0.25}$$

To find p, divide 10.50 by 0.25

$$p = 42$$

Dawanna can buy 42 pencils for $3.50.

Guided Practice

1. A copy machine made 35 copies in 2 minutes. How long will it take to make 700 copies?

Let m stand for the number of minutes it takes to make 700 copies.

a. Complete the proportion:

$$\frac{35}{2} = \underline{\hspace{3cm}}$$

b. Use the cross-products rule:

$$\underline{\hspace{3cm}} \times \underline{\hspace{3cm}} = \underline{\hspace{3cm}} \times \underline{\hspace{3cm}}$$

c. Solve the equation for m.

$$m = \underline{\hspace{3cm}}$$

Exercises

Choose the proportion that matches the problem. Then solve.

2. In 30 minutes, Pedro can walk 2 miles. How many miles can he walk in 90 minutes?

Let x represent the number of miles he can walk in 90 minutes.

a. $\dfrac{30}{2} = \dfrac{x}{90}$ **b.** $\dfrac{30}{90} = \dfrac{x}{2}$ **c.** $\dfrac{30}{2} = \dfrac{90}{x}$

Number of miles: _____

3. Jamal read 45 pages of his book in 2 hours. How many pages can he read if he has 8 hours to read this weekend?

Let p represent the number of pages he can read in 8 hours.

a. $\dfrac{45}{2} = \dfrac{p}{8}$ **b.** $\dfrac{45}{2} = \dfrac{8}{p}$ **c.** $\dfrac{45}{} = \dfrac{8}{p}$

Number of pages: _____

Solve each problem.

4. It cost $55 to run a small ad in the local paper for 3 days. How much would it cost to run the ad for 12 days?

_____

5. The day care center has a child-to-adult ratio of 9:2. How many children can be at the center if there are 8 adults?

_____

Application

6. Use counters or paper slips of two different colors. Model the ratio 2:3. Use the manipulatives to model several other ratios that are equal to it. For example, 4 green counters and 6 blue counters use the ratio of 2:3.

 USING PROPORTIONS TO SOLVE PROBLEMS

Reminder

A proportion is a statement that two ratios are equal.

Reminder

In a proportion, the cross-products are equal.

Problem 1: A recipe for apple spice muffins calls for 3 apples to make 12 muffins. How much will it cost to buy enough apples for 60 muffins if apples cost $.25 each?

To solve this problem, you must use 2 steps.

Step 1
Write and solve a proportion to find how many apples are needed.

Let a represent the number of apples needed for 60 muffins.

$$\frac{3}{12} = \frac{a}{60}$$

$$3 \times 60 = 12 \times a$$

$$180 = 12 \times a$$

$$a = 180 \div 12$$

$$a = 15 \text{ apples}$$

Step 2
Multiply the number of apples by $.25.

$$\begin{array}{r} 15 \\ \times\ 0.25 \\ \hline 75 \\ 30 \\ \hline \$3.75 \end{array}$$

The cost of apples for 60 muffins is $3.75.

Problem 2: When Margarita left home, the odometer on her car read 53,246. After 3 hours of driving, the odometer read 53,385. At this rate, how many hours will it take her to complete a trip of 400 miles?

Step 1
Subtract to find the number of miles she has driven in 3 hours.

$$\begin{array}{r} 53{,}385 \\ -\ 53{,}246 \\ \hline 139 \text{ miles} \end{array}$$

Step 2
Write and solve a proportion. Let h represent the number of hours a 400-mile trip takes.

$$\frac{139}{3} = \frac{400}{h}$$

$$139 \times h = 3 \times 400$$

$$139 \times h = 1200$$

$$h = 1200 \div 139$$

Use a calculator:

$$h = 8.633093525$$

The trip will take about 8.6 hours.

1. Find the time in hours and minutes it will take a copier to make 2,000 copies if it makes 40 copies in 3 minutes.

   a. Find the total time in minutes. Let m represent the number of minutes it takes to make 2,000 copies.

   $$\frac{40}{3} = \frac{2,000}{m}$$

   $$40 \times m = 6,000$$

   $$m = \underline{\hspace{2cm}}$$

   b. Find the number of hours by dividing the number of minutes by 60.

   $$60\overline{\smash{)}\hspace{2cm}}$$

   _____ hours _____ minutes

Exercises

2. When Tyrell started typing, it was 3:40. When he finished typing 5 pages, it was 4:30. At that rate, how long will it take him to type 25 pages?

_____

4. It took Dave 2 hours to drive 95 miles. He must still drive 70 miles to Ames and then 150 miles to Blinton. At that rate, how long will the rest of his trip take?

_____

6. Janeen's recipe for nut bread calls for 3 cups of flour and makes 2 loaves. She will sell her bread for $1.50 per loaf at a fair. How much can Janeen earn at the fair if she has 9 cups of flour on hand?

_____

3. At lunch, 2 quarts of milk can serve 6 children. How many gallons of milk will be needed to serve 42 children? (Hint: 4 quarts = 1 gallon)

_____

5. Yoshiko can read 25 pages in one hour. She must read a 750-page book. She can read for 2 hours a day. How many days will it take her to read the book?

_____

7. A casserole that serves 5 people calls for 2 cups of rice. There are 8 cups of rice in a sack. How many sacks of rice are needed to make enough casserole for 60 people?

_____

Application

8. What generalizations can you make about how to recognize types of problems that you can use a proportion to solve?

_____

_____

USING DATA FROM TABLES

Vocabulary

data: information

Reminder

LPs are long-playing records. EPs are extended-play records.

Reminder

A million dollars is $1,000,000.

This table shows the total list price value of recordings shipped to stores for three different years. The information in this table is called **data**.

Millions of Dollars, Shipments of Recordings

Type	1991	1992	1993
Singles (records)	63.9	66.4	51.2
LPs/EPs	29.4	13.5	10.6
CDs	4,337.3	5,326.5	6,511.4
Cassettes	3,019.6	3,116.3	2,915.8
Cassette singles	230.4	298.8	298.5
CD singles	35.1	45.1	45.8
Music videos	118.1	157.4	213.3

[*Source*: 1995 Information Please Almanac, p. 742]

When you are asked questions about a table, it is a good idea to look over the whole table first. Read the title of this table, "Millions of Dollars, Shipments of Recordings." Then read the column heads and the labels for each row.

How many dollars worth of CD singles were shipped in 1992?

To find the answer, find the entry across from the label "CD singles" and under the heading "1992." The number in the table is 45.1. However, this number represents millions of dollars.

$$45.1 \times 1,000,000 = 45,100,000$$

So, $45,100,000 worth of CD single recordings were shipped in 1992.

Guided Practice

1. What was the dollar value of music video shipments in 1993?

   a. Write the entry in the table that is across from "Music videos" and down from "1993."

   _____

   b. Change the number you found in **a** to millions of dollars:

   _____ $\times$ 1,000,000 = $ _____

Use the table "Millions of Dollars, Shipments of Recordings."

2. According to the table, in what year did CD shipments have the greatest dollar value?

_____

3. How many dollars worth of LPs and EPs were shipped in 1991?

_____

Use the table below to solve the following problems. The table shows the results of a survey taken over the phone by a radio station.

Radio Station Survey—Most Popular Music

Favorite Type of Music	Number of People
Rock	215
Country	175
Rap	81
Classical	102
Pop	342
Jazz	85
Total surveyed:	1,000

4. What was the most popular form of music among the people who took part in the survey?

_____

5. How many more people liked country than liked jazz?

_____

6. Which form of music is popular with about 10% of the people who took part in the survey? $(10\% = \frac{1}{10})$

_____

7. What one form of music is just about as popular as rap and jazz combined?

_____

COOPERATIVE
LEARNING

8. In a small group, decide on a survey you can take. Have every person collect data from as many people as they can. Put the data together in a table. Then list some questions that can be answered with the data in your table.

USING DATA FROM TABLES TO SOLVE PROBLEMS

Reminder

When you need information from a table, be sure to read the title and labels on the table.

Reminder

To find what percent one number is of another, divide the amount by the base. Change the decimal or fraction to a percent.

The table below gives some information about TV sets in U.S. households.

Television Set Ownership

Homes That Have . . .	Number
One set	32,028,000
Two or more sets	62,172,000
Cable	59,346,000

Find the percent of total homes with TV that have cable.

This problem must be done in two steps. First, find the total number of homes with TV. You can find this by adding the number of homes with one set to the number of homes with 2 or more sets.

$$\begin{array}{r} 32,028,000 \\ +\ 62,172,000 \\ \hline 94,200,000 \end{array}$$

Next, find what percent of all the homes with TV have cable.

number of homes with cable: 59,346,000

$$percent = amount \div base$$
$$= 59,346,000 \div 94,200,000$$

Use a calculator:

59,346,000 ÷ 94,200,000 = 0.63 = 63%

63% of homes with TV have cable.

Guided Practice

1. Of all the homes with TVs, 93,258,000 have color TVs. What percent of the homes have only black-and-white TVs?

   a. Find the number of homes with only black-and-white TVs.

Total homes with TVs: 94,200,000

Total homes with color TVs: 93,250,000

Homes with only black-and-white TVs: _____

 b. Find the percent of all homes with TV that have only black-and-white TV.

Divide your answer to part **a** by 94,200,000. Use a calculator.

_____ ÷ 94,200,000 = _____

c. Write your answer to part **b** as a percent. _____

Exercises

The Shirt Superstore is having a sale. Cashiers use this table for figuring out the correct discount for each item in the store.

Shirt Code	Discount
A100-C230	10%
D500-E305	20%
F25-G125	30%
H420-J980	40%

2. What is the selling price of a shirt labeled A120 that has a regular price of $16.50?

3. What is the selling price of a shirt labeled F70 that has a regular price of $25?

Each cassette, CD, and video in the music store is given a letter code. The table below shows the price for each coded item.

Cassettes		CDs		Videos	
Code	Price	Code	Price	Code	Price
AX	$5.99	GR	$14.99	TW	$10.50
AY	$6.99	GS	$15.99	TX	$15.50
AZ	$7.99	GT	$16.99	TY	$19.50
AB	$8.99	GU	$17.99	TZ	$25.00

4. How much change will Tran get from a $20 bill if he buys a cassette labeled AX and one labeled AZ and also pays $.75 in tax?

5. Abdul has a discount coupon for 15% off. How much will he pay for 2 videos labeled TY? (This price will not include sales tax.)

Application

COOPERATIVE
LEARNING

6. Work in small groups. Look at the music store table. Each group member should make up one problem that can be solved using the table. Then discuss and solve each problem.

USING DATA FROM GRAPHS

Vocabulary

bar graph: a graph that compares quantities by using bars of different lengths

axis: a number line along which measurement information is arranged. A bar graph usually has a vertical axis and a horizontal axis.

circle graph: a graph that compares quantities by showing what part of the whole each quantity represents

Reminder

In a graph, it is important to include labels so that the graph can be read.

A **bar graph** compares data by using bars of different lengths to represent the data. This graph shows the number of T-shirts sold at Amy's Shirts last week, grouped by color. Notice that the vertical axis, or number line, is labeled from 0 to 240 to show the number of T-shirts sold. The horizontal axis is labeled to show the different colors of T-shirts sold.

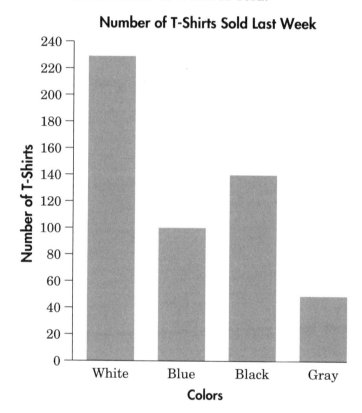

Amy sells white T-shirts for $5 each and color T-shirts for $7 each. How much money did she receive for selling white T-shirts last week?

To solve this problem, find the number of white T-shirts sold. You can find out by looking at the bar labeled "white." Find the top of the bar and read across to the vertical axis. The bar ends just halfway between 220 and 240, so Amy sold 230 white T-shirts. The problem states that she sold them for $5 each.

$$230 \times \$5 = \$1150$$

Amy earned $1150 from selling white T-shirts last week.

Monthly Budget

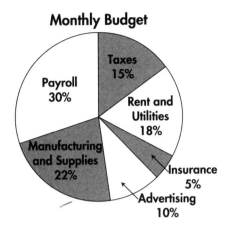

Reminder

There are 360° in a circle.

Another kind of graph is called a **circle graph**. It shows how quantities relate to a whole. This circle graph shows a breakdown of the monthly expenses of Art to Wear, a T-shirt company.

The size of each section of the graph reflects how large a part of the budget goes for that expense. For instance, since 30% of the budget is for payroll, that section of the circle is 30% of the whole graph.

1. Suppose the monthly budget is $38,000. How much money a month will be used for payroll?

Find 30% of the total monthly budget.

$38,000 \times 0.3 =$ _____

Exercises

Use the bar graph in this lesson to solve.

2. How many more black shirts than gray shirts did Amy sell last week?

_____

3. Suppose Amy reduces the price of color T-shirts to $4. If she sells the same number of blue shirts next week, how much will she make on blue shirts next week?

_____

Use the circle graph in this lesson to solve. Remember that the company's total monthly budget is $38,000.

4. How much money does the company spend on advertising each month?

_____

5. What is the combined percentage of the company budget that is spent on rent and utilities and manufacturing and supplies?

_____

Application

COOPERATIVE LEARNING

6. Find a bar graph or circle graph in a newspaper, almanac, or other source. Work with your group to make up a list of questions that can be answered by using data from this graph. Exchange graphs and questions with another group. Work together to answer the other group's questions.

USING DATA FROM GRAPHS TO SOLVE PROBLEMS

Vocabulary

line graph: a graph formed by plotting points for data and drawing lines that connect the points

Reminder

To find data in graphs, read the labels on the graph carefully.

This graph shows how many lawns Jake mowed each day during 1 week in June.

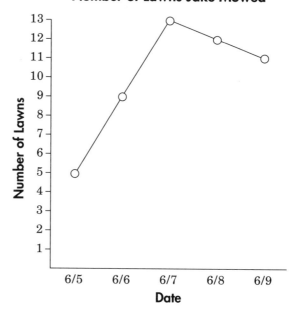

Number of Lawns Jake Mowed

Jake earns $8 per lawn. How much more money did he earn on June 8 than on June 6?

You must solve this problem in two steps.

First, find the amount of money he earned both days:

June 8: 12 × $8 = $96

June 6: 9 × $8 = $72

Next, subtract to find how much more he earned on June 8.

$96 − $72 = $24 more

Guided Practice

1. How much money did Jake earn all week?

   a. First, find the total number of lawns he mowed:

   _____ + _____ + _____ + _____ + _____ = _____

b. Then, find the total amount he earned:

_____ × \$8 = _____

Exercises

The bar graph below shows the difference in average weekly earnings between men and women. The data is arranged by age group.

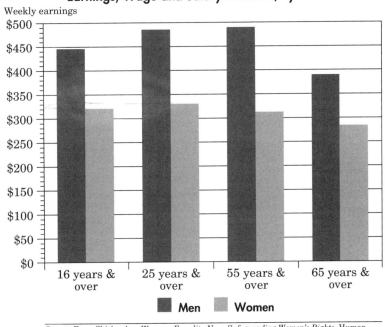

The Male-Female Wage Gap: Average Weekly Full-Time Earnings, Wage and Salary Workers, by Sex: 1988

Source: From Shirley Ann Wagner, *Equality Now: Safeguarding Women's Rights*, Human Rights series, p. 54. Vero Beach, Fla.: Rourke Corp., 1992.

2. How much more are the average *yearly* earnings of men 16 years and over compared with those of women 16 years and over?

(Hint: 52 weeks = 1 year.) _____

3. Suppose a 34-year-old woman earns \$25,000 a year. How much more does she earn per year than the average *yearly* earnings for a woman

her age? _____

Application

COOPERATIVE
LEARNING

4. Work with a partner. Look back at the problem about Jake's lawn mowing. You were asked to find how much more money he earned on June 8 than on June 6. Can the problem be solved a different way from the one that was presented in the lesson? Write a paragraph explaining another way to find how much more Jake earned on June 8 than on June 6.

CONSTRUCTING GRAPHS BASED ON DATA

The table below shows the amount of sales of a new can opener over the past few months. Graph the missing data. Use the graph to estimate the amount of sales in May.

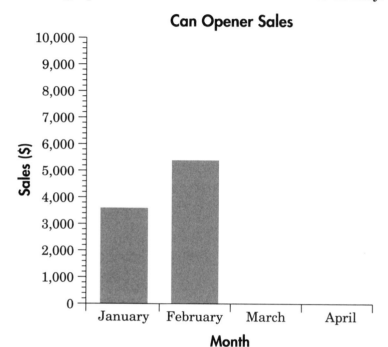

Can Opener Sales

Month	Sales ($)
Jan.	$3,600
Feb.	$5,400
Mar.	$7,500
Apr.	$9,500

Since sales increase each month by about $2000, a reasonable estimate for May is $9,500 + $2,000 = $11,500.

Guided Practice

1. The circle graph on the next page shows the Wu family's budget. It uses data from the table.

		Percent of Total	Circle Angle
Food	$600	19%	67°
Rent	$1200	37%	135°
Car	$450	14%	50°
Other Transportation	$150		
Savings	$320		
Other	$480		
Total	$3200		

a. Find the entry for Other Transportation. Divide the money amount by the total budget, $3200. Round to the nearest percent. Write the percent in the table.

$150 ÷ $3200 = _____%

b. The Circle Angle column will help you find the size of the angle you must draw to show that section of the circle. To find the angle for Other Transportation, multiply 360° by the percent you just found. (Change the percent to a decimal for multiplying.) Round your answer to the nearest degree.

360° × 0. _____ = _____ °

c. Use a protractor to draw the angle. Label the section.

Exercises

2. Complete the table and the circle graph of the Wu family's budget. What is the size in degrees of the section showing Savings?

_____

3. On what item does the family spend 15% of its money?

_____

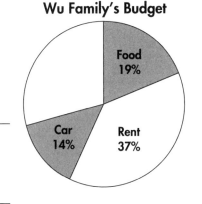

Wu Family's Budget

Food 19%
Rent 37%
Car 14%

Complete the bar graph using the data below. Use the graph to predict how many listeners radio station WPOP will have in December.

Month	Listeners
Aug.	35,000
Sept.	30,000
Oct.	24,900
Nov.	20,000

4. Estimated number of listeners for December:

_____

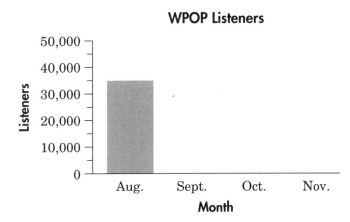

WPOP Listeners

Application

5. Write a paragraph explaining how you would decide whether to make a bar graph or a circle graph for a set of data. What kinds of subjects are suitable for each kind of graph?

 CONSTRUCTING GRAPHS TO SOLVE PROBLEMS

Reminder

Graphs are pictures of data.
Sometimes graphs can indicate trends.
A line graph uses connected points to show trends.

The table shows how Davon's hourly wage has changed. Look at the line graph of the data. Predict how much Davon will make per 35-hour week after his next raise.

	Wage
Year	**per hour**
1992	$7.25
1993	$7.75
1994	$8.25
1995	$8.80
1996	$9.30

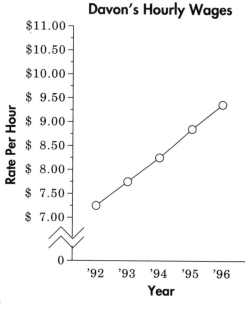

From the graph, you can see that Davon's wage has increased steadily each year. Each year the raise was either $.50 or close to $.50. A good estimate for his next raise is $9.30 + $.50 = $9.80.

Reminder

The zigzag lines above the zero on the graph show that the numbers from zero to $7.00 have been left out. This saves space but keeps the graph in proportion.

To find his salary for a 35-hour work week at that rate, multiply:

$$\$9.80 \times 35 = \$343.00$$

You can also imagine extending the line graph to predict in what year Davon will make at least $11 per hour. If this trend continues, he will probably be making $11 per hour in four years.

Guided Practice

1. Laquana earns $2500 per month. The partly completed table below shows her monthly expenses. If her car payment doubles, what percent of her budget will the new car payment make up?

Item	Amt	Percent	Angle
Rent	$500	20%	72°
Phone/Utilities	$125	5%	18°
Car	$200		
Other	$1675	67%	

a. Make a circle graph to see the effect. Complete the table. Use it to create the graph on the right.

b. Draw a dashed line on the completed graph to show how much more of her budget would be taken by a car payment that is twice as big.

c. What percent of her budget will the bigger car payment make up?

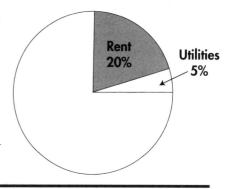

_____

2. Varleyville has a minor league baseball team. The table shows some weekly attendance figures. Complete the line graph.

Week ending	Attendance
April 20	8,000
April 27	10,000
May 4	14,000
May 11	22,000

3. What might attendance figures be for the next week?

_____

4. Do you think the attendance figures will rise in the same way all season? Explain your answer.

_____

_____

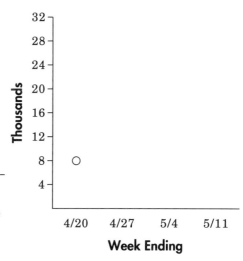

Game Attendance

Thousands

32
28
24
20
16
12
8
4

4/20   4/27   5/4   5/11

Week Ending

Application

COOPERATIVE
LEARNING

5. Work with a partner. Find the scores or attendance figures of your favorite team for the last week. Graph the results. Discuss together any conclusions you can draw from your graph.

FINDING AREA AND PERIMETER

Vocabulary

perimeter: the distance around a figure

area: the inside region of a figure

Reminder

A rectangle has two pairs of equal sides. A square has four equal sides.

Reminder

To estimate, round the numbers you are using.

Diop wants to enclose a rectangular plot for growing vegetables. He wants the plot to be 10 meters long and 5 meters wide. How much fencing will he need?

The diagram at the right shows Diop's plot. To find the amount of fencing he needs, find the **perimeter** of the rectangle. The perimeter is the distance around the rectangle:

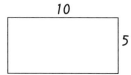

$$10 + 5 + 10 + 5 = 30$$

For the perimeter of a rectangle, you can use this formula:

$$P = 2l + 2w$$
where l is length and w is width.
$$P = (2 \times 10) + (2 \times 5)$$
$$P = 20 + 10 = 30$$

Diop will need 30 meters of fence for his plot.

In order to know how much fertilizer to buy for his plot, Diop will need to know the **area**. Area is the inside region of a figure. It is measured in square units.

In this diagram, you can see the area of Diop's plot marked off in square meters.
The area is 50 square meters.

The formula for the area of a rectangle is $A = l \times w$.

$$A = 10 \times 5$$
$$A = 50$$

Diop will need enough fertilizer for 50 square meters.

Guided Practice

1. Ileana wants to do a large square painting for an art exhibit. The painting will be 7 feet on each side. How many feet of wood will she need to frame this painting?

a. Draw a diagram. Does Ileana need to find the perimeter or the area?

Draw your diagram here:

b. Find the measure Ileana needs.

_____

c. Write the correct label for your answer—feet or square feet.

_____

Exercises

2. Haing wants new carpeting for his room. His room measures 12 feet by 14 feet. How many square feet of carpeting must he order?

_____

3. Alberto will cover a countertop with 1-foot square tiles. His countertop is 3 feet wide and 3 feet long. How many tiles will he need?

_____

4. Dahlia wants to put weatherstripping around the window in her room. The window measures 36 inches by 48 inches. How much weatherstripping does she need?

_____

5. Marina plans to put wood molding around a piece of plywood that is 44.1 cm long and 38.9 cm wide. How much molding will she need?

 _____

6. The diagram at the right shows the floor plan of an office. An electrician must run a wire from point A to point B. How much wire will the electrician need?

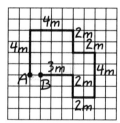

_____

Application

7. Suppose you are moving into a new house. Give two examples of situations in which you must find the perimeter in order to build or repair something. Give two examples of situations in which you must find area in order to build or repair something.

SOLVING AREA AND PERIMETER PROBLEMS

Reminder

To change a smaller measuring unit such as inches to a larger unit such as feet, divide. To change a larger measuring unit such as feet to a smaller measuring unit such as inches, multiply.

Reminder

12 in. = 1 ft
3 ft = 1 yd
36 in. = 1 yd

Reminder

144 sq in. = 1 sq ft
9 sq ft = 1 sq yd

Jaconda wants carpeting for her room, which measures 10 feet by 12 feet. Carpeting is sold by the square yard. How many square yards of carpeting does she need?

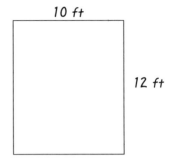

This problem can be solved in two steps. First, find the area of the room.

$$Area = l \times w$$
$$= 10 \times 12 = 120 \text{ square feet}$$

Then, change the square feet to square yards.

Since 1 square yard is the same as 9 square feet and since square feet are smaller than square yards, divide 120 by 9.

$$120 \text{ square feet} \div 9 = 13\tfrac{1}{3} \text{ square yards}$$

Jaconda also wants a wallpaper border all around her room where the ceiling meets the walls. The border costs $5.20 a foot. How much will the border cost?

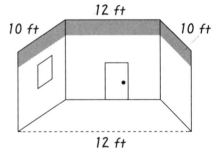

To find the cost, first find out how much she needs. You need to find the perimeter of the room.

$$Perimeter = 2l + 2w$$
$$= 2 \times 12 + 2 \times 10$$
$$= 24 + 20 = 44 \text{ feet}$$

Then, multiply by $5.20 to find the cost.

$$\begin{array}{r} \$5.20 \\ \times\ 44 \\ \hline \$228.80 \end{array}$$

The border will cost $228.80.

1. How many feet of fence will be needed to go around a garden that measures 20 yards by 30 yards?

   a. First, find the perimeter of the garden.

   $P = 2l + 2w$

   $= \underline{\hspace{2cm}}$ yards

   b. Then, change yards to feet. Multiply the answer in part **a** by 3.

   $\underline{\hspace{2cm}}$ yards $\times$ 3 $=$ $\underline{\hspace{2cm}}$ feet

Exercises

2. The vinyl flooring that Charel wants costs $18.25 per square yard. How much will Charel pay to cover a kitchen floor that is 3 yards long and 2 yards wide?

3. A company is carpeting 12 offices. Each office measures 3 yards by 4 yards. Carpeting costs $21.50 per square yard. What is the total cost?

4. Lace trim costs $5.99 per yard. How much will it cost to trim the border of a tablecloth that is 1.5 yards long and 0.6 yards wide?

5. Wood for picture frames is sold by the foot. How many feet are needed to frame a picture that is 15 inches by 10 inches?

6. A can of paint can cover 400 square feet. Lamark knows that 3 of his walls measure 325 square feet in all. The last wall is 8 feet high and 10.5 feet wide. Is one can enough paint for all 4 walls?

7. Yuriko's garden measures 15 yards by 30 yards. The bag of fertilizer she bought will cover 1000 square yards. What percent of the bag should she use in her garden?

Application

COOPERATIVE LEARNING

8. Work in a small group. Suppose you have 100 feet of fencing.

   a. List all the different rectangles you can make from this fencing. Use whole numbers for the lengths and widths.

   b. Which of these rectangles will give you the largest area? How do you know?

FINDING THE MEAN, MEDIAN, AND MODE

Vocabulary

mean: average of a set of numbers

median: middle number in a set of numbers

mode: number in a set of data which appears most often

Amiri wants to get part-time work as a cashier. This is what five different local stores pay per hour:

$$\$5.50, \ \$5.25, \ \$6.20, \ \$5.75, \ \$6.20$$

Amiri decided to find the mean, median, and mode of the data to get some idea of what she can expect as a typical rate.

The **mean** is the average of a set of data. It is found by adding all the data and dividing by the number of items.

$$Mean = (5.50 + 5.25 + 6.20 + 5.75 + 6.20) \div 5$$

$$28.90 \div 5 = \$5.78$$

The **median** is the middle number. Half the numbers are greater than the median, and half are less than the median. To find the median, arrange the numbers in order. Then find the middle.

$$Median: \ 5.25, \ 5.50, \ 5.75, \ 6.20, \ 6.20$$

$\uparrow$ $\$5.75$ is the median.

If the number of numbers is even, the median is the average of the two middle numbers.

Reminder

Some sets of numbers have no mode. Here is an example: 5, 2, 3, 4.

The **mode** is the number that appears most often. Here, $6.20 appears twice. So, the mode is $6.20.

Suppose Amiri is offered a cashier's job that pays $5.35. Since that amount is less than the mean, the median, and the mode, Amiri knows she can probably do better than that somewhere else.

Guided Practice

1. Here are Nazir's point scores in 10 basketball games:

    20, 34, 28, 19, 34, 35, 29, 29, 21, 29

    a. Find the mean.

    $(20 + 34 + 28 + 19 + 34 + 35 + 29 + 29 + 21 + 29) \div 10$

    _____ $\div 10 = $ _____

b. Find the median.

Arrange in order:

_____ _____ _____ _____ _____ _____ _____ _____ _____ _____

↑   ↑   Find the average of these two.

Median: _____

c. Find the mode.

The number of points that appears most often is _____.

Exercises

Find the mean, median, and mode for each set of data.

2. Jari got the following scores on his math tests:
82, 80, 88, 94, 80, 86, 88, 90, 92, 88

Mean: _____   Median: _____   Mode: _____

3. Here are the yearly salaries of the employees in the customer service department:
$23,500, $25,000, $24,700, $25,000, $40,000, $23,000, $24,000

Mean: _____   Median: _____   Mode: _____

4. Hitomi has been practicing her long jump for the track meet. These are her last 5 distances:
5.7 m, 5.8 m, 5.5 m, 6 m, 5.9 m

Mean: _____   Median: _____   Mode: _____

5. These are the ages of the workers in the packaging department:

23, 19, 20, 25, 37, 20, 42, 63, 55, 32, 41

Mean: _____   Median: _____   Mode: _____

Application

COOPERATIVE
LEARNING

6. Suppose you have 10 numbers. The median, the mean, and the mode are all 10. Give a set of numbers for which all those statements can be true. There is more than one correct answer to this problem! Can you come up with more than one set of numbers? (Hint: What do you know about the sum of the 10 numbers?)

USING MEAN, MEDIAN, AND MODE

Problem 1: The mean age of the workers in Division A of a company is 34.2. In Division B the ages of the workers are 20, 42, 36, 21, 19, 39 and 25. How much older or younger is the average (mean) age in Division B than in Division A? Round answers to the nearest tenth.

You need to solve this problem in two steps.

a. Find the mean of the ages in Division B. You can use a calculator if you want.

$$20 + 42 + 36 + 21 + 19 + 39 + 25 = 202$$

$$202 \div 7 = 28.85714286 \text{ or } 28.9$$

b. Compare the mean age with the given mean for Division A. The mean age of Division B is younger. Subtract to find out how much younger.

$$34.2 - 28.9 = 5.3$$

The Division B employees are, on average, 5.3 years younger than the Division A employees.

Problem 2: Ten years ago, the median age of workers in Division B was 22. How much older or younger is the median age of workers in that division today?

a. Find the median age by ordering the ages correctly.

$$19, 20, 21, 25, 36, 39, 42$$

b. Compare the two median ages and subtract.

$$25 - 22 = 3$$

The median age today is 3 years older.

Guided Practice

1. Dr. Lopez's receptionist kept track of how much time the doctor spent with each of 10 patients one day:

4 min, 10 min, 6 min, 11 min, 8 min,

20 min, 7 min, 9 min, 12 min, 15 min

Based on the mean time spent with each patient, how many patients can Dr. Lopez see in 4 hours?

a. Find the mean time per patient:

$(4 + 10 + 6 + 11 + 8 + 20 + 7 + 9 + 12 + 15) \div 10 = $ _____

b. Change 4 hours to minutes: $4 \times 60 = $ _____

c. Divide the minutes by the mean time per patient:

_____ ÷ _____ = _____

Exercises

2. Carmen sells earrings that she makes. Each pair costs her $4 to make. She sells each pair for $10. Here are her records for the last four weeks:

Week ending	4/5	4/12	4/19	4/26
Number of pairs sold	55	60	43	62

Find her average profit per week. (Profit = price − cost)

_____

3. Yung found out that the mean time it took to register a car at the Motor Vehicles office was 25 minutes. It takes him 15 minutes to drive to the Motor Vehicles office. If he leaves his house at 2:15 pm, when can he expect to return after driving to Motor Vehicles, registering his car, and driving back home?

_____

4. Here is a record of how many hours a day Manuel worked in the supermarket last week: 7 h, 7.5 h, 9 h, 8.5 h, 9 h, 6.5 h, 4 h

Use the median of this data to estimate how much he earns in a month. He works 25 days a month and earns $9.50 an hour.

_____

Application

5. Kaleem heard that the average weekly salary at a local printing business was $630 a week. Then, he found out that 4 of the 5 employees earn only $350 per week.

a. How much does the fifth employee earn per week? _____

b. An average isn't always the best way to describe a typical value in a set of data. Write a paragraph explaining how to avoid being fooled by statistics.

_____

FINDING THE PROBABILITY FOR A SIMPLE EXPERIMENT

Vocabulary

probability: a measure of how likely a particular result is

experiment: a process that is conducted to see what the results will be. In an experiment most of the conditions are planned or known, and one unknown element is being investigated.

outcome: one possible result of an experiment

Reminder

A ratio is a way of comparing numbers.

Jamie is playing a game. When it is her turn, she throws a number cube to see how many spaces she can move. She wants to get a 6 on the next throw. What is the probability?

A number cube has 6 sides, numbered 1 through 6. Throwing the number cube is called an experiment. An **experiment** is a process you conduct to see what the results will be. Usually you are trying to find out what will happen to just one factor or element. The different possible results are called outcomes. In the case of the number cube, the outcomes are 1, 2, 3, 4, 5, or 6. The probability of getting 6 is the measure of how likely it is that 6 will be the outcome. The probability is the ratio of the number of favorable outcomes to the number of possible **outcomes**. Remember that you can express a ratio as 1:6 or $\frac{1}{6}$.

The **probability** of getting $6 = \frac{1}{6}$ or 1 in 6, since there is one way of getting 6 and there are 6 possible outcomes.

In probability problems, it is common to write P(6) to mean the probability of getting a 6.

$$So, \ P(6) = \frac{1}{6}$$

Remember, the probability of getting a 6 doesn't change with the number of times you throw the cube. *Each* time you throw, the probability of getting a 6 is 1 in 6.

Another type of probability experiment is spinning a spinner. The spinner at the right has 8 possible outcomes. What is the probability of getting an E if you spin the spinner once?

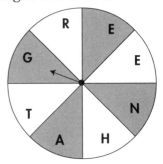

The letters on the spinner are G R E E N H A T. Notice that there are two Es. The number of favorable outcomes is 2. The number of possible outcomes is 8, since there are 8 equal sections on the spinner.

$$P(E) = \frac{2}{8} \text{ or } \frac{1}{4}$$

Guided Practice

1. An envelope contains five index cards. On each card is one of these numbers: 2, 4, 7, 10, or 21. A card is drawn without looking. What is the probability that it is an even number?

   a. How many possible outcomes are there?_____

   b. How many favorable outcomes are there? (In other words, how many even numbers are in the envelope?)_____

   c. P(even number) = $\dfrac{\text{Number of favorable outcomes}}{\text{Number of possible outcomes}}$ = _____

   = _____

Exercises

Find each probability.

Experiment A: Each letter of the word MISSISSIPPI is written on a slip of paper and placed in an envelope. A slip of paper is chosen without looking.

2. P(M) = _____ **3.** P(I) = _____ **4.** P(P) = _____

Experiment B: The spinner at the right is spun once.

5. P(Lose a turn) = _____

6. P(Free turn) = _____

Experiment C: A bag contains 4 white marbles, 8 blue marbles, and 3 green marbles.

7. P(White) = _____ **8.** P(Blue) = _____ **9.** P(Green) = _____

10. P(White or blue) = _____ **11.** P(Purple) = _____

Application

12. Suppose you throw a single 6-sided number cube whose sides are numbered 1 through 6. What is the probability of getting a number less than 10? Think of and describe three more probabilities that will have the same value.

_____

FINDING THE PROBABILITY FOR A COMPOUND EVENT

Vocabulary

event: a result of an experiment

sample space: a list of all the possible outcomes of an experiment

compound event: the result of two experiments

Reminder

The probability of an event is the ratio of the number of favorable outcomes to the number of possible outcomes. This ratio can be expressed as a fraction reduced to the lowest common denominator.

Reminder

A coin tossed by itself would have a $\frac{1}{2}$ probability of landing heads up. A die rolled by itself would have a $\frac{1}{6}$ probability of landing on any one number (such as 4).

A **compound event** is the result of two experiments. For example, if you toss a coin and then roll a die, you can get the following results.

Toss a coin	Roll a die
H (for heads)	1
H	2
H	3
H	4
H	5
H	6
T (for tails)	1
T	2
T	3
T	4
T	5
T	6

There are 12 possible outcomes of this compound experiment. The list of possible outcomes is called the **sample space** of the experiment.

The probability of getting heads on the coin and 3 on the die, P(H, 3), is $\frac{1}{12}$ since there is only one possible way to get heads and 3.

Here are some other probabilities for this experiment:

$$P(T, even\ number) = \frac{3}{12}\ or\ \frac{1}{4}$$

$$P(H, number\ less\ than\ 3) = \frac{2}{12},\ or\ \frac{1}{6}$$

$$P(T, not\ 6) = \frac{5}{12}$$

Guided Practice

1. Suppose two coins are tossed. What is P(H, H)?

   a. Write the sample space (all the possible outcomes) for this experiment:

b. How many outcomes on this list include two heads?_____

c. What is the total number of possible outcomes?_____

d. P(H, H) = _____

**Find each compound event and list the sample space
(all the possible outcomes). Then find the probabilities.**

Experiment A: Toss a coin and then choose a card from an envelope
with 3 cards, each with letter A, B, or C.

2. Sample space: _____

3. P(T, A) = _____   **4.** P(H, not C) = _____

Experiment B: Roll two number cubes.

5. Sample space:

_____

_____

6. P(1, 1) = _____   **7.** P(2, even) = _____

8. P(4, number less than 5) = _____   **9.** P(odd, not 3) = _____

Experiment C: Roll a number cube and spin the spinner.

10. P(4, S) = _____

11. P(1, T) = _____

12. P(even, not U) = _____

13. P(not 2, V) = _____

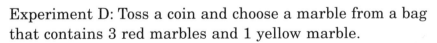

Experiment D: Toss a coin and choose a marble from a bag
that contains 3 red marbles and 1 yellow marble.

14. P(H, red) = _____   **15.** P(T, yellow) = _____

Application

COOPERATIVE

LEARNING

16. Work with a partner or small group. Design two experiments involving
probability of compound events. Then, for one event, do your
experiment 100 times. How do the results match what you expected
based on probability?

COMPUTING WITH INTEGERS

Vocabulary

integer: a positive or negative whole number

Reminder

You can also think of positive as up and negative as down, as they appear on many thermometers.

Yianna looked at the outside thermometer at 6:00 A.M. The thermometer read ⁻4°. At noon, the thermometer read 12°. How many degrees warmer was it at noon than at 6:00 A.M.?

The numbers ⁻4 and 12 are examples of **integers**. Integers are positive and negative whole numbers. Positive numbers are greater than 0; negative numbers are less than 0. A number line can help you understand integers.

Notice that negative integers are to the left of 0 on the number line, and positive integers are to the right of 0. The numbers increase in value from left to right. So, ⁻5 is less than ⁻2.

Using the number line, you can see that there are 16 units between ⁻4 and 12. Therefore, at noon, the temperature was 16° warmer than at 6:00 A.M.

Negative integers can be used to represent money owed, yards or points lost, distance below sea level, and many other real-life situations.

Nand keeps track of his money using integers. He owed his brother $10. Then he got $15 for his birthday. How much does he actually have now?

Nand records owing his brother $10 as ⁻10 and getting $15 as ⁺15.

The number line can be used to show the result of adding ⁺15 to ⁻10.

Start with ⁻10. Move 15 units in the plus direction.

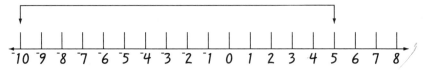

The result is 5. So, Nand now has $5.

1. In a football game, the home team was on their own 40-yard line. Their object was to get the ball to their opponents' end zone. Then a penalty of 10 yards was called against the team. What is the home team's new position?

   a. Write the 10-yard penalty as an integer. _____

   b. On the number line below, start with 40 on the home team's side. Move 10 in the negative direction.

   c. What is the team's position now?

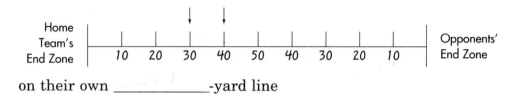

   on their own _____-yard line

Exercises

Use integers to help you solve these problems.

2. Graciela owes the bank $350. Then she pays the bank $210. Write an integer for the amount of debt she now has.

   _____

3. Roberto owed his sister $20. Then he borrowed another $15 from her. Write an integer for the money he owes her now.

   _____

4. An oil rig extends 10 ft below the sea and 45 ft above the sea. What is its full length?

   _____

5. The home team was on their own 30-yard line. Then they got a 20-yard penalty. Where are they now?

   _____

6. At 3:30 A.M. it was ⁻5°. Then the temperature rose 14°. What was the temperature after that rise?

   _____

7. The temperature was 7°. Then it fell 10°. What was the temperature after that drop?

   _____

Application

COOPERATIVE
LEARNING

8. Work with a partner. Explain how a number line can be used to solve Exercise 4. Then, describe three additional real-life situations that can be solved by adding integers.

SOLVING PROBLEMS WITH INTEGERS

Reminder

Integers are positive and negative whole numbers.

Reminder

On a number line, positive is to the right, negative is to the left.

The temperature at 9:00 P.M. was 10°. Then it started falling at the rate of 2° per hour. What was the temperature after 8 hours?

You must solve this problem in two steps.

First, find out how much the temperature dropped in 8 hours.

$$2° \times 8 \ hours = 16°$$

To find the new temperature, subtract 16° from 10°.

Think of a number line: Start with 10, and go 16 in the negative direction:

The result is ⁻6. So, the temperature after 8 hours was ⁻6°.

Here is another example:

The temperature was 7° at midnight and ⁻11° by 6:00 A.M. At what rate did the temperature drop during those 6 hours?

First, find the amount of the drop. On a number line, find out how many degrees are between 7° and ⁻11°.

There are 18° degrees in between the two points.

Next, divide the number of degrees by 6 hours to find the rate per hour.

$$18 \div 6 = 3$$

So, the temperature dropped at a rate of 3° per hour.

1. Gloria's regular weekly take-home pay is $375. This week she also earned $156 in overtime pay. She had $389 in expenses through the week. How much money did she have left at the end of the week?

   a. First, find Gloria's total pay for the week.

   Add 375 + 156 = _____

   b. Then, find what is left after expenses.

   _____ − 389 = _____

Exercises

2. A club's account had a negative balance of $500. Then the 9 club members each put the same amount of money into the account. As a result, the account now has a positive balance of $175. What was the amount that each club member put into the account?

   _____

3. Cara's salary is $350 per week. Taxes of $53.45 are taken out of this amount. A health insurance payment of $12 is also taken out. This week, Cara received a $50 bonus. What was her take-home pay this week?

   _____

4. The temperature is now 3°. It is dropping by 4° per hour. What will the temperature be after 5 hours?

   _____

5. The temperature was ⁻10° at 5:00 A.M. and 4° by 7:00 A.M. By how many degrees per hour did the temperature increase?

   _____

Application

6. Stocks on the stock market rise or fall in value by fourths and halves of points or by whole points. Stocks from each company are listed according to the value per share of stock. One day, stock of the Dazzle Clothing Corporation closed at $13\frac{1}{4}$. So each share of stock was worth $13.25. The next day, that stock closed at $12\frac{1}{2}$.

   a. What was the change in the value of the stock?

   _____

   b. Harry owns 200 shares of stock in the Dazzle Clothing Corporation. How much money did he lose when this stock changed in value?

   _____

Solve.

1. Jared bought a book for $9.95 and a magazine for $2.50. How much did he spend in all?

_____

2. Leila bought 14.1 gallons of gasoline at $1.57 per gallon. How much did the gasoline cost?

 _____

3. Gloria gave the cashier a $5 bill for her $3.75 lunch. How much change did she receive?

_____

4. Ty bought 2 shirts at $15 each and a pair of slacks for $24. What was the total cost before sales tax?

_____

5. Raul had $543.12 in the bank. He made a deposit of $27, and the bank paid him $4.32 interest. What is his new balance?

_____

6. Inez had $342.56 in the bank. She made a withdrawal of $85.90. What is her new balance?

_____

7. Shaunee's bank account had a balance of $8,947.28 on April 25. During the next two days, she made the following deposits and withdrawals. Find the new balance after the April 27 withdrawal.

Date	Withdrawal	Deposit	Balance
April 26	$321.00	$67.90	
April 27	$65.35		_____

Estimate.

8. Sam bought cassette tapes that cost $11.99, $10.50, $9.99, $7.25, and $5.50. About how much did he spend in all before sales tax?

_____

9. Juana earns $561.23 per week. About how much does she earn per year? (1 year = 52 weeks) _____

COOPERATIVE **LEARNING**

10. In a small group, discuss how you decide which operation to use to solve a problem. Write a summary of your discussion that tells how you decide that a problem can be solved by adding. Do the same for the other operations.

_____

_____

 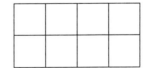

5-8 CUMULATIVE REVIEW

Solve.

1. Pablo drove for $3\frac{3}{4}$ hours. Write the time as a decimal.

_____

2. Sue bought $2\frac{3}{8}$ yards of fabric. Write the amount as a decimal.

_____

3. Mei Li walked $2\frac{1}{2}$ miles from work to the store and $3\frac{3}{4}$ miles back home. How much did she walk in all?

_____

4. Edward had 12 feet of tubing. He used $4\frac{2}{3}$ feet. How many feet does he have left?

_____

5. Isamu bought a table on sale for 25% off. The regular price of the table was $150. What was the amount of the discount?

_____

6. Tamika bought a plant for $6.50. The sales tax is 2%. How much sales tax must she pay?

_____

 7. Carmen bought a picture frame that cost $14.99. What was the total cost including $3\frac{1}{2}$% sales tax?

_____

8. Kareel gets $82.50 a week from his part-time job. He is going to get a 6% raise. How much will he make a week when he gets the raise?

_____

Estimate.

9. James must mail packages that weigh $4\frac{1}{2}$ oz, $12\frac{1}{4}$ oz, $8\frac{1}{2}$ oz, and $9\frac{5}{8}$ oz. About how much do the packages weigh in all? _____

10. A new car costs $12,349.26. The sales tax is 5%. About how much will the sales tax on this car be? _____

 11. Draw a diagram showing how to add $\frac{3}{4} + \frac{1}{8}$ using these fraction models:

9-12 CUMULATIVE REVIEW

Solve.

1. A shirt with a regular price of $18 is on sale for $3.60 off. What is the percent of the discount? _____

2. Alta was charged $.63 sales tax for a dress costing $21. What is the percent of the sales tax? _____

3. Tamika bought a VCR for $260 with tax included. The price before tax was $250. What percent sales tax did she pay? _____

4. Sara bought a book for $17.50 that has a regular price of $25. What percent discount did she get? _____

5. The computer has been working on a problem for 18 minutes. The screen says the job is 40% complete. How long will the whole job take?

   _____

6. Radhika bought a car for 80% of the regular price. She paid $6,400. What was the regular price of the car? _____

7. Victor has saved $300. This is 60% of the money he needs for his vacation. How much more money does he need to save? _____

8. Rajeen wants to save 10% of his salary each week. He makes $375 per week. How much will he save in 5 weeks? _____

9. There are three different kinds of percent problems. You can look for the amount of the percent, the rate of the percent, or the base. Which kind of problem would usually give the greatest number as an answer? Why?

   _____

   _____

   _____

Choose the correct equation and solve the problem.

1. Tyrell has 127 cassette tapes. At the beginning of the summer he had 98 tapes. How many tapes has he bought this summer?

   Let t represent the number of tapes he got this summer.

   a. $t + 127 = 98$ **b.** $t + 98 = 127$ **c.** $t \times 98 = 127$

   Number of tapes he got this summer: _____

2. Tickets to the ball game cost \$15 each. The community center has \$120 set aside to buy tickets. How many tickets can they buy?

   Let t represent the number of tickets they can buy.

   a. $120 \div 15 = t$ **b.** $t + 15 = 120$ **c.** $120 \times 15 = t$

   Number of tickets they can buy: _____

Use an equation to help you solve each problem.

3. Ali bought 4 pens and a binder. The binder cost \$3.50. Not including sales tax, his bill was \$7.30. How much did each pen cost?

   _____

4. Ved scored 30 points in a game by making 12 field goals and some three-point shots. How many three-point shots did he make? (Field goals: 2 points; three-point shots: 3 points)

   _____

Write a problem for each equation.

5. $x + 4.25 = 8.90$

   _____

   _____

6. $25q = 775$

   _____

   _____

7. $20 - r = 12.40$

   _____

   _____

8. $\dfrac{36}{t} = 4$

   _____

   _____

9. Write a paragraph explaining how to write an equation for a word problem.

_____

_____

1. In 40 minutes, Josefina can read 25 pages of her book. How many pages can she read in 2 hours? (1 hour = 60 minutes)

2. A recipe calls for $1\frac{1}{2}$ cups of sugar and 2 cups of flour. How much sugar will you need if you increase the recipe and use 8 cups of flour?

3. Wesley can walk 2 miles in 40 minutes. He leaves his house at 8:15 and walks 6 miles. What time is it when he finishes?

4. Phil can type 3 pages in 35 minutes. He must type a report that has 24 pages. He has already typed 9 pages. How much longer will he take to type the rest?

This table tells the number of people registered at the Language Center for classes.

Language	Day Classes	Night Classes
Spanish	45	123
Chinese	21	83
French	56	25
Portuguese	11	9
Vietnamese	23	76
Korean	21	32

5. How many people in all are registered for Spanish classes?

6. How many fewer people take French at night than during the day?

7. How many more people have registered for Vietnamese than for Korean?

8. How many more people take night classes than take day classes?

COOPERATIVE LEARNING

9. Form small groups. Each group member should make up a problem about a recipe that can be solved by using a proportion. Each group member should solve every other member's problem, showing the proportion used to solve the problem.

1. How many more homes were built from 1991 to 1995 than from 1985 to 1990?

_____

2. How many more homes were built in the peak year than in the lowest year?

_____

3. What was the percent decrease in home-building in 1992 compared with 1991?

_____

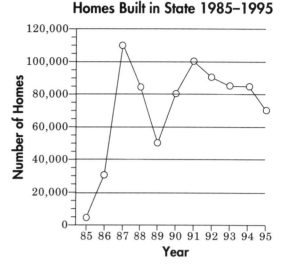

Homes Built in State 1985–1995

4. How many more homes were built in 1995 than in 1985? _____

5. Use the data in the table on the left to complete the circle graph on the right. Then answer the questions.

Employees at Green Market

Experience	Percent	Angle
less than 1 yr	25	90°
1-2 yrs	25	90°
2-3 yrs	30	
3-5 yrs	15	
over 5 yrs	5	

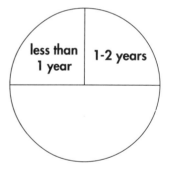

6. What percent of the employees have 2 years or less of experience?

_____

7. If there are 200 employees, about how many have 3 or more years of experience? _____

8. Look back at the graph you completed for problem 5. Write 2 questions that can be answered using the graph.

_____

_____

_____

1. Isamu's garden is 50 meters long and 30 meters wide. What is the area of the garden?

_____

2. Maria Luisa has a square painting that measures 4 feet on each side. How much wood does she need to make a frame for the painting?

_____

3. Shakti has a rectangular tablecloth that measures 54 inches by 72 inches. How many yards of ribbon does she need to make a border for it?

_____

4. Oscar's room measures 8 feet by 10 feet. How many square yards of wall-to-wall carpeting does he need for his room? (9 sq. ft = 1 sq. yd)

_____

5. Jellal has done the following number of sit-ups per day in the past 5 days: 43, 46, 48, 45, 48. Find the following:

Mean: _____

Median: _____

Mode: _____

6. The price of cantaloupe at several different fruit markets was $.89, $1.29, $.95, $1.39, $1.45, and $1.09. Find the following:

Mean: _____

Median: _____

Mode: _____

7. These are the weekly salaries that workers earn at Kool Klothing Outlet: $240, $310, $290, $235, $220, and $350. The median salary for workers at Midland Clothing is $247. How much more *per year* is the median salary at Kool Klothing? (1 year = 52 weeks)

_____

8. Work with your group to make up a room and decide on its size. Make a room plan and label the measurements of the floor, the walls, and the ceilings. Also draw in at least 1 door and 1 window and label their measurements. Suppose you were painting all the walls. Find the number of square feet of surface that would be painted. How many cans of paint would be needed? (Assume that a can of paint covers 400 square feet.)

_____

Find the probability.

Experiment A: A cube is rolled. The numbers on the cube are 1, 2, 3, 4, 5, and 6.

1. Probability of rolling 3:

2. Probability of rolling a number less than 6:

Experiment B: A coin is tossed, and the number cube is rolled.

3. Probability of getting heads and 4:

4. Probability of getting tails and an even number:

Experiment C: The number cube is rolled, and a name is picked from a hat. The names in the hat are Amy, Ben, Sally, and George.

5. Probability of getting 1 and Sally's name:

6. Probability of getting an odd number and a boy's name:

Solve these problems.

7. Jari is $25 in debt. Then she makes $40. How much does she have after paying her debt? _____

8. The football team was at the 25-yard line. They lost 10 yards on the next play and gained 8 yards after that. Where are they now?

_____

9. The temperature increased by 2° an hour from midnight until 9:00 A.M. At 9:00 A.M. the temperature was 12°. What was the temperature at midnight? _____

10. At a carnival, there are two games of chance. In the first, a player spins a wheel divided into 28 equal sections. Equal numbers of sections are painted red, blue, green, and yellow. The player wins if the wheel lands on red. In the second game, a ball is hidden under 1 of 5 shells. The shells are mixed, and the player has to guess which shell the ball is under. If the games are run honestly, which one offers the player the best chance of winning? Explain your answer.

_____

_____

_____

ANSWER KEY

LESSON 1 (pages 2–3)
  1. $51; no   **3.** $15; $5 + $7 + $3 = $15
  5. $66; 54 + 12 = 66
  7. $31.50; 5.25 × 6 = 31.50
  9. $63.37; 24.99 + 14.79 + 23.59 = 63.37
  11. Possible answer:
    Round to the nearest dollar, ten dollars, or other amount to ensure that the amount does not exceed the amount you have.

LESSON 2 (pages 4–5)
  1. a. $10.50 **b.** $9.50
  3. $5.10; 3.45 + 6.70 + 11.00 + 3.75 = 24.90;
    30 − 24.90 = 5.10
  5. $196.55; 37 × 6.85 = 253.45;
    450.00 − 253.45 = 196.55
  7. yes; 42.50 rounds to 40, 36 rounds to 40,
    20.95 rounds to 20; 40 + 40 = 80, 110 − 80
    = 30, so he should have enough money.
  9. Assuming that a 3-item lunch is juice, salad and either hot lunch or sandwich, there are 31 lunches less than $7: any lunch that includes soup (9) or burger (9) or a cheese sandwich (9); burrito, apple or orange juice and green salad or coleslaw (4); no combinations with turkey or deluxe sandwiches will be less than $7.

LESSON 3 (pages 6–7)
  1. a. 372.50; 114.23 **b.** $486.73
  3. $832.52; 635.14 + 197.38 = 832.52
  5. $595.19; 845.19 − 250 = 595.19
  7. $600; 400 + 200 = 600
  9. Outcomes of game will vary.

LESSON 4 (pages 8–9)
  1. a. $260.80 **b.** $144.60
  3. $561.23; 25 + 123.50 = 148.50; 709.73 −
    148.50 = 561.23
  5. $4146.90; 4623.82 + 2831.75 − 167 −
    3090.50 + 35.63 − 86.80 = 4146.90
  7. Possible answer: add the deposits together and add the total to the balance to get a new balance. Then, add the withdrawals. Subtract the total withdrawal from the new balance. *Or:* add or subtract each transaction in the order it occurs to keep track of the checks and have a record that is in time order.

LESSON 5 (pages 10–11)
  3. 0.3; 3 ÷ 10 = 0.3   **5.** 0.375; 3 ÷ 8 = 0.375
  7. 12.75 hours; 3 ÷ 4 = 0.75
  9. about 18 lb; 8 + 5 + 5 = 18

LESSON 6 (pages 12–13)
  1. a. $\frac{2}{8}$ **b.** $\frac{3}{8}$ **c.** $\frac{4}{8}$ or $\frac{1}{2}$ yd
  3. $\frac{3}{4}$ hour; $1\frac{1}{2} = 1\frac{2}{4}$, $\frac{1}{4} + 1\frac{2}{4} = 1\frac{3}{4}$; $2\frac{1}{2} = 2\frac{2}{4} = 1\frac{6}{4}$;
    $1\frac{6}{4} − 1\frac{3}{4} = \frac{3}{4}$
  5. about $266; 7 + 8 + 8 + 7 + 8 = 38;
    38 × $7 = 266

LESSON 7 (pages 14–15)
  1. a. 0.12 **b.** 15 × 0.12 = 1.80; $1.80
  3. $6.00; 29.99 × 0.20 = 5.998
  5. $7.84; 49 × 0.16 = 7.84 For problem 7, accept other reasonable estimates based on different rounded numbers.
  7. $140; 2000 × 0.07 = 140
  9. $.08; 4 × 0.02 = 0.08
  11. $4.80; 8 × 0.60 = 4.80
  13. Yes; 60% is more than one half, therefore you will pay less than half the original price.

LESSON 8 (pages 16–17)
  1. a. $5.10 **b.** $28.90   **3.** $134.25; 179 × 0.25
    = 44.75; 179.00 − 44.75 = 134.25
  5. $28.40; 35.50 × 0.20 = 7.10; 35.50 − 7.10 =
    28.40   **7.** $320; 400 × 0.20 = 80; 400 − 80
    = 320; $302.14 is also acceptable.
  9. First pair: 49 × 0.20 = 9.80;
    49 − 9.80 = 39.20
    Second pair: 35 × 0.15 = 5.25; 35 − 5.25 =
    29.75; the first pair still costs more.
    Calculators can help with comparison shopping because you can find the exact selling prices and compare them.

LESSON 9 (pages 18–19)
  1. a. 0.20 **b.** .20 = 20%
  3. 5%; 1.20 ÷ 24 = 0.05
  5. 25%; 15 ÷ 60 = 0.25   **7.** 24%; 12 ÷ 50 = 0.24
  9. 18%; 10 ÷ 54.99 = 0.1818512457
  11. Sample answer: Divide the amount of the discount by the original price. Then, change your decimal answer to a percent by moving the decimal point two places to the right.

LESSON 10 (pages 20–21)
  1. a. 7.20 **b.** 7.20 ÷ 24 = 0.30 **c.** 30%
  3. 5%; 37.80 − 36 = 1.80; 1.80 ÷ 36 = 0.05
  5. 3.0%; 23.48 − 22.80 = 0.68,
    0.68 ÷ 22.80 = 0.0298245614
  7. 30%; 35 − 24.50 = 10.50, 10.50 ÷ 35 = 0.30
  9. 3.7%; 34.20 − 32.99 = 1.21, 1.21 ÷ 32.99 =
    0.0366777811   **11.** Answers will vary.

LESSON 11 (pages 22–23)
  1. a. 0.01 **b.** 20 ÷ 0.01 = 2000 **3.** 20; 16 ÷ 0.80
    = 20 **5.** $5.21; 1.25 ÷ 0.24 = 5.20833 . . .
  7. 1050; 21 ÷ 0.02 = 1050 **9.** 800 mg;
    8.8 ÷ 0.011 = 800 **11.** Problems will vary.

LESSON 12 (pages 24–25)
  1. a. 4 **b.** $4.00 \div 0.80 = 5$
  3. $119; $21 \div 0.15 = 140, 140 - 21 = 119$
  5. $90; $8 \div 0.40 = 20; 20 \times 4.50 = 90$
  7. $550; $2288 \div 0.08 = 28,600,$
    $28,600 \div 52 = 550$
  9. 105 minutes; $45 \div 0.30 = 150,$
    $150 - 45 = 105$

LESSON 13 (pages 26–27)
  1. a. B $(s \div 6 = 25)$ **b.** 150; $25 \times 6 = s$
  3. 288; $12 \times 24 = c; 12 \times 24 = 288$

LESSON 14 (pages 28–29)
  1. a. 15; $31 - 16 = 15$ **b.** 3; $15 \div 5 = 3$
  3. $.75; $10 - 6.25 = 3.75, 3.75 \div 5 = 0.75$
  5. $135; $420 \div 2 = 210, 210 - 75 = 135$
  7. 46 points; $50 - 27 = 23, 23 \times 2 = 46$

LESSON 15 (pages 30–31)
  1. How many nickels does Jill have?
    Sample answer is given for 3.
  3. Maria has $40,000 in two bank accounts.
    One account has $15,000. How much is in
    the other account?
  5. Problems and equations will vary. It should
    be possible to solve the problems using the
    given equations.

LESSON 16 (pages 32–33)
  1. How many tickets were in each book that
    she sold?
  3. Sample answer: The same number of seats
    are in Studio A and in Studio B. There are
    500 seats in Studio C. The total capacity of
    all three studios is 800 people. How many
    can sit in Studio A? **5.** Answers will vary.

LESSON 17 (pages 34–35)
  1. a. $\frac{700}{m}$ **b.** $35 \times m = 2 \times 700$ **c.** 40; $2 \times 700 =$
    $1400, 1400 \div 35 = 40$ **3.** A, 180;
    $2p = 45 \times 8 = 360, 360 \div 2 = 180$
  5. 36; $\frac{9}{2} = \frac{x}{8}, 2x = 9 \times 8 = 72, x = 72 \div 2 = 36$

LESSON 18 (pages 36–37)
  1. a. 150, $6000 \div 40 = 150$ **b.** 2 h 30 min; 150
    $\div 60 = 2.5$ **3.** $3\frac{1}{2}$ gal; $\frac{2}{6} = \frac{x}{42}, 6x = 84,$
    $x = 84 \div 6 = 14, 14 \div 4 = \frac{14}{4} = 3\frac{2}{4} = 3\frac{1}{2}$
  5. 15 days; $\frac{25}{1} = \frac{750}{x}, 25x = 750, x = 750 \div 25 =$
    $30, 30 \div 2 = 15$ **7.** 3; $\frac{5}{2} = \frac{60}{x}, 5x = 120,$
    $x = 120 \div 5, x = 24, 24 \div 8 = 3$

LESSON 19 (pages 38–39)
  1. a. 213.3 **b.** $213.3 \times 1,000,000 = 213,300,000$
  3. $29,400,000 **5.** 90; $175 - 85 = 90$
  7. Country; $81 + 85 = 166$

LESSON 20 (pages 40–41)
  1. a. 950,000 **b.** $950,000 \div 94,200,000 =$
    0.0100849257 **c.** 1%
  3. $17.50; $25 \times 0.30 = 7.50, 25 - 7.50 = 17.50$
  5. $33.15; $2 \times 19.50 = 39, 39 \times 0.15 = 5.85,$
    $39.00 - 5.85 = 33.15$

LESSON 21 (pages 42–43)
  1. 11,400 **3.** $400; 100×4
  5. 40%; $18 + 22 = 40$

LESSON 22 (pages 44–45)
  1. a. $5 + 9 + 13 + 12 + 11 = 50$
    b. $50 \times $8 = 400
    For problem 3, answers based on rounded
    readings of earnings from the graph are
    also acceptable.
  3. $7580; $335 \times 52 = 17,420,$
    $25,000 - 17,420 = 7580$

LESSON 23 (pages 46–47)
  1. a. 5% **b.** 18°
    c. Your graph should show a section of 18°
  3. Other **5.** Answers will vary. You might
    have said that a bar graph is best at
    comparing data, while a circle graph is
    best at showing parts of a whole.

LESSON 24 (pages 48–49)
  1. 16%; **a.** Phone/Utilities, 5°, 18°; Car, 8%,
    29° (rounded from 28.8°); Other, 241° **b.**
    You should have drawn a dashed line
    that doubles the area given to car payment
    to 58°. **c.** 16%.
  3. About 30,000 if this pattern continues.
  5. Answers will vary.

LESSON 25 (pages 50–51)
  1. a. perimeter **b.** 28, $4 \times 7 = 28$; **c.** 28 feet
  3. 9; $3 \times 3 = 9$
  5. 166 cm; $2 \times 44.1 + 2 \times 38.9$
  7. Answers will vary. Possible answers:
    area—carpeting or vinyl flooring;
    perimeter—weatherstripping around
    windows and doors; molding, wiring.

LESSON 26 (pages 52–53)
  1. a. 100 yd; $2 \times 20 + 2 \times 30 = 100$
    b. $100 \times 3 = 300$
  3. $3096; $3 \times 4 = 12; 12 \times 12 = 144;$
    $144 \times 21.50 = 3096$
  5. $4\frac{1}{6}$ ft; $2 \times 15 + 2 \times 10 = 50; 50 \div 12 = 4\frac{1}{6}$
  7. 45%; $15 \times 30 = 450; 450 \div 1000 = 0.45$

LESSON 27 (pages 54–55)
   1. a. $278 \div 10 = 27.8$ **b.** 19, 20, 21, 28, 29, 29, 29, 34, 34, 35—29; #5 and #6 got 29 and 29 respectively. **c.** 29
   3. Mean: $26,457.14, $185,200 \div 7 =$ 26,457.14286; Median: $24,700; Mode: $25,000
   5. Mean: 34.2, $377 \div 11 = 34\frac{3}{11}$; Median: 32; Mode: 20

LESSON 28 (pages 56–57)
   1. a. 10.2, $102 \div 10 = 10.2$ **b.** 240
   c. $240 \div 10.2 = 23.52$, about 23 patients
   3. 3:10 pm; $25 + 15 + 15 = 55$, 2h 15 min + 55 min = 2 h 70 min = 3 h 10 min
   5. a. $1750, $630 \times 5 = 3150$, $350 \times 4 = 1400$, $3150 - 1400 = 1750$ **b.** Answers will vary.

LESSON 29 (pages 58–59)
   1. a. 5 **b.** 3 **c.** $\frac{3}{5}$ **3.** $\frac{4}{11}$ **5.** $\frac{2}{6}$ or $\frac{1}{3}$ **7.** $\frac{4}{15}$
   9. $\frac{3}{15}$ or $\frac{1}{5}$ **11.** none

LESSON 30 (pages 60–61)
   1. a. (H,H), (H,T), (T,H), (T,T) **b.** 1 **c.** 4 **d.** $\frac{1}{4}$
   3. $\frac{1}{6}$ **5.** (1,1), (1,2), (1,3), (1,4), (1,5), (1,6), (2,1), (2,2), (2,3), (2,4), (2,5), (2,6), (3,1), (3,2), (3,3), (3,4), (3,5), (3,6), (4,1), (4,2), (4,3), (4,4), (4,5), (4,6), (5,1), (5,2), (5,3), (5,4), (5,5), (5,6), (6,1), (6,2), (6,3), (6,4), (6,5), (6,6) **7.** $\frac{3}{36}$ or $\frac{1}{12}$
   9. $\frac{15}{36}$ or $\frac{5}{12}$ **11.** $\frac{1}{24}$ **13.** $\frac{5}{24}$ **15.** $\frac{1}{8}$

LESSON 31 (pages 62–63)
   1. a. $^-10$ **b.** move on the number line from 40 to 30 **c.** 30 yd **3.** $^-$35, $^-20 + ^-15 = ^-35$
   5. on their own 10-yard line; $30 - 20 = 10$
   7. $^-3°$, $7 - 10 = ^-3$

LESSON 32 (pages 64–65)
   1. a. 531 **b.** $531 - 389 = 142$; $142 left
   3. $334.55, $350 + 50 = 400$, $^-53.45 + ^-12 = ^-65.45$, $400 + ^-65.45 = 334.55$
   5. 7°, from $^-10$ to 4 is 14, $14 \div 2 = 7$

CUMULATIVE REVIEW: LESSONS 1–4 (page 66)
   1. $12.45; $9.95 + 2.50$
   3. $1.25; $5.00 - 3.75 = 1.25$
   5. $574.44; $543.12 + 27 + 4.32 = 574.44$
   7. $8628.83; $8947.28 - 321 = 8626.28 + 67.90 = 8694.18 - 65.35 = 8628.83$
   For problem 9, other reasonable estimates based on different rounded numbers are acceptable.
   9. $30,000; $600 \times 50 = 30,000$

CUMULATIVE REVIEW: LESSONS 5–8 (page 67)
   1. 3.75 h; $\frac{3}{4} = 3 \div 4 = 0.75$
   3. $6\frac{1}{4}$ mi; $2\frac{1}{2} = 2\frac{2}{4}$, $2\frac{2}{4} + 3\frac{3}{4} = 5\frac{5}{4} = 6\frac{1}{4}$
   5. $37.50; $150 \times 0.25 = 37.50$
   7. $15.51; $14.99 \times 0.035 = 0.52465$,

$14.99 + 0.52 = 15.51$
   9. 36 oz; $5 + 12 + 9 + 10 = 36$
   11. Your diagram should show 3 fourths shaded, 1 eighth shaded, and an answer showing 7 eighths shaded.

CUMULATIVE REVIEW: LESSONS 9–12 (page 68)
   1. 20%; $3.60 \div 18 = 0.20$
   3. 4%; $260 - 250 = 10$, $10 \div 250 = 0.04$
   5. 45 min; $18 \div 0.40 = 45$
   7. $200; $300 \div 0.60 = 500$, $500 - 300 = 200$
   9. The base would probably give the greatest number, because that is the whole number of which the percent is only a part.

CUMULATIVE REVIEW: LESSONS 13–16 (page 69)
   1. b. 29; $127 - 98 = 29$
   3. $.95; $7.30 - 3.50 = 3.80$, $3.80 \div 4 = 0.95$
   Sample answers are given for 5 and 7.
   5. Ava bought a paperback book for $4.25 and a poster. Her total bill was $8.90. How much did the poster cost?
   7. Mia gave the clerk $20 for a sandwich and got $12.40 in change. How much did the sandwich cost?
   9. Possible answer: Find the known numbers in the problem. Let a letter stand for the unknown number. Decide whether you must add, subtract, multiply, or divide using the known numbers to find the unknown number.

CUMULATIVE REVIEW: LESSONS 17–20 (page 70)
   1. 75 pp, $\frac{40}{25} = \frac{(2 \times 60)}{x}$, $40x = 3000$, $x = 75$
   3. 10:15, $\frac{2}{40} = \frac{6}{x}$, $2x = 240$, $x = 120$, $120 \div 60 = 2$ h, 8:15 + 2 hours = 10:15
   5. 168, $45 + 123$
   7. 46, $23 + 76 = 99$, $21 + 32 = 53$, $99 - 53 = 46$
   9. Answers will vary.

CUMULATIVE REVIEW: LESSONS 21–24 (page 71)
   1. 70,000, 1991–1995: 430,000, 1985–1990 = 360,000, $430,000 - 360,000 = 70,000$
   3. 10%, $100,000 - 90,000 = 10,000$, $10,000 \div 100,000 = 0.1$
   5. 108°, 54°, 18°
   7. 40, $15\% + 5\% = 20\%$, $200 \times 0.2 = 40$

CUMULATIVE REVIEW: LESSONS 25–28 (page 72)
   1. 1500 sq m, $50 \times 30 = 1500$
   3. 7 yd, $2 \times 54 + 2 \times 72 = 252$, $252 \div 36 = 7$
   5. 46, $230 \div 5 = 46$; 46, 48 **7.** $936, $(240 + 290) \div 2 = 265$, $265 - 247 = 18$, $18 \times 52 = 936$

CUMULATIVE REVIEW: LESSONS 29–32 (page 73)
   1. $\frac{1}{6}$ **3.** $\frac{1}{12}$ **5.** $\frac{1}{24}$ **7.** $15, $^-25 + 40 = 15$
   9. $^-6°$, $9 \times 2 = 18$, $12 - 18 = ^-6°$